MAKING
SIX SIGMA
LAST

MAKING SIX SIGMA LAST

Managing the Balance Between Cultural and Technical Change

GEORGE ECKES

JOHN WILEY & SONS, INC.

New York • Chichester • Weinheim • Brisbane • Singapore • Toronto

Published by John Wiley & Sons, Inc.
Published simultaneously in Canada.

This publication is designed to provide accurate and authoritative information in regard to the subject matter covered. It is sold with the understanding that the publisher is not engaged in rendering professional services. If professional advice or other expert assistance is required, the services of a competent professional person should be sought.

Library of Congress Cataloging-in-Publication Data:

Eckes, George, 1954–
    Making Six Sigma last : managing the balance between cultural and technical change / George Eckes.
        p.   cm.
    ISBN 0-471-41548-0 (cloth : alk. paper)
    1. Organizational change—Management.   2. Corporate culture.
    3. Leadership.   I. Title: Managing cultural and technical change.   II. Title.
HD58.8 .E275 2001
658.4'06—dc21

                                                              2001017549

Printed in the United States of America.

10   9   8   7   6   5   4   3   2   1

To Father Ted Hesburgh,
who through change
made this a better world

Foreword

The axiom now made famous is that change is the only constant in life, and the rate of change is accelerating. While this is true, it should also be noted that while change is inevitable, both organizations and the people in it can experience significant growth from a comprehensive change management process that addresses both the "what to change" and the "how to gain organizational acceptance."

This book shares the voyage of those who have pursued a Six Sigma management philosophy in order to create a lasting Six Sigma culture in their companies. They know it is an arduous task to obtain the type of results demonstrated by General Electric or AlliedSignal.

Making Six Sigma Last: Managing the Balance Between Cultural and Technical Change, is the book that will help you achieve a Six Sigma cultural transformation, quicker, easier, and more effectively than you will without it.

Six Sigma is for most organizations a major change from how they typically manage their business. Movement toward managing with fact and data and aggressively pursuing greater efficiencies and effectiveness is a dramatic change. Change, even the positive change associated with Six Sigma, will be resisted.

George Eckes, noted author, and consultant, is well aware of this resistance. George has been a successful business consultant for over twenty years and he has a background in clinical psychology. This experience and background gives him a unique insight into the strategic, technical, and cultural challenges confronting an organization attempting to implement Six Sigma. In his first book, *The Six Sigma Revolution: How General Electric and Others Turned Process Into Profits,* George addressed the strategic and tactical elements of Six Sigma. In pragmatic fashion, he reviewed how both management and professional contributors need to create and maintain a more effective and efficient organization that will lead to greater long-term growth and profitability.

While many books on Six Sigma talk about the tactics of Six Sigma, George addressed the strategy of Six Sigma so that management clearly understood how to create and maintain Six Sigma as an ongoing management philosophy. In this book, George addresses what no other Six Sigma consultant addresses, how to create a Six Sigma culture.

First, let me tell you what this book is not about. It is not about the tactics of Six Sigma. It is not about chartering teams, creating data collection plans, measurement of sigma performance or generating solutions to drive Six Sigma improvements. All of those concepts were covered in George's first book. Instead, this book is exclusively devoted to creating the acceptance of Six Sigma, which is the pivotal element to making Six Sigma a cultural phenomenon in your organization and making it last, not just the short term costs savings program it is for so many organizations.

In the early chapters of *Making Six Sigma Last,* George specifies that the need for Six Sigma must be established. Specific details and ideas are shared with the reader around what will happen to an organization if Six Sigma is not adopted. These are the threats to an organization. These threats are great short term motivators. However, threats, real or imagined, can only sustain motivation to Six Sigma for so long. In addition to threats, George shares his experiences with the opportunities that await an organization that adopts a Six Sigma management philosophy.

Once the need is created and the organization starts to implement the ideas found in George's first book, resistance is certain to occur. In Chapter 3, George addresses the four major types of resistance to Six Sigma. Once identified, he then practices the tools of Six Sigma to share the root causation for each type of resistance, and the solutions that can soften or eliminate the resistance so that there is greater buy in to the Six Sigma initiative in your organization.

In Chapter 4, he shares with the reader the various vision statements of his many clients. He then goes on to share ideas on how an organization new to the Six Sigma philosophy can create their own, unique vision of Six Sigma, complete with the mindset, results and behaviors that should accompany your new management philosophy.

In Chapter 5, George discusses how the systems and structures of an organization must change so that Six Sigma can thrive. Like tilling the soil for seed planting, George specifies how to hire, develop, and reward those in your organization attempting to achieve Six Sigma as a cultural phenomenon. He shares his teaching secrets that make him among the most successful Six Sigma consultants today. He provides specific suggestions on how to communicate the Six Sigma initiative, both to the internal audience and the outside world of stockholders and the public at large.

In Chapter 6, George shares a unique methodology to gage how well your organization has implemented the technical aspects of Six Sigma, as well as how well Six Sigma is being accepted in your organization. This mathematical formula to determine where you are currently in your Six

Sigma journey, and the probability of your ultimate success is perhaps the highlight of this book. He helps you not only calculate your overall Six Sigma implementation score, but segments where your strengths and weaknesses are in both the tactics and the acceptance of those tactics. He shares five case studies of successes and failures of those attempting to implement Six Sigma.

As he does in *The Six Sigma Revolution*, George finishes this book with ten pitfalls to avoid in the pursuit of making Six Sigma last. Just as he did in his first book, George attempts to share his years of experience with both his successful and less than successful clients so that you don't end up like the latter.

We at Lithonia Lighting, have utilized many of the techniques and concepts found in both of George's books to improve our performance. You will find this the most important book on your business book shelf, whether your change effort is Six Sigma or something else. George's writing style is like his lectures; detailed, pragmatic, example driven, and most of all, useful. You will find this book easy to read, and difficult to implement, but without it, your attempts at implementing a lasting Six Sigma culture will be much more difficult and lengthy. I highly recommend this book to all business leaders who want to create Winning Businesses for their customers, employees and shareholders.

Jack Becker
Vice President, Six Sigma
Lithonia Lighting
Conyers, Georgia

Preface

Six Sigma is the management philosophy that is sweeping the world by storm. Created first by Motorola in the 1980s, then popularized by AlliedSignal and General Electric (GE) in the 1990s, Six Sigma has more than proven its worth to organizations attempting to improve their productivity and profitability.

Unfortunately, many organizations attempting to implement this cutting edge philosophy are not generating the type of success that GE and AlliedSignal have accomplished.

While there are several root causes for the lackluster performance of some organizations, this book will focus on the major reasons why so many organizations are not maximizing their Six Sigma investment.

Plainly and simply, a host of organizations that are jumping on the Six Sigma bandwagon are expecting a panacea. Like any popular approach to improving productivity, Six Sigma improvement tools and techniques are sound, principled, and effective. However, like most popular approaches toward improvement, the technical elements are only half the story. Implementing Six Sigma in an organization will result in the organization managing with fact and data. This approach will be a dramatic change for many organizations that ran their businesses based on anecdotal approaches and the opinion of the person highest on the organizational chart.

Implementation of any change effort within an organization is difficult. However, compounding the difficulty with Six Sigma is the level of associated comprehensive tools and techniques. Resistance is a natural, often genetic reaction to any change in our lives. Unmanaged and unaddressed, the resistance to Six Sigma will spell the downfall of the effort.

Thus, *Making Six Sigma Last* focuses on the necessary management activities that will help create the balance between the technical elements of Six Sigma necessary for improved productivity and the cultural elements that will make the technical more effective.

As Six Sigma becomes more popular, resistance to it will grow. While most people claim the opposite, I am of the opinion that more people will see Six Sigma as more fad than reality. Thus, this book is devoted to those that want to gain acceptance to Six Sigma throughout their organization.

We begin with how to create the need for Six Sigma. Creating the need means first uncovering the threats to an organization if they *don't* implement Six Sigma. While these threats can initially begin the acceptance of Six Sigma, uncovering the *opportunities* for an organization if they *do* implement Six Sigma can be far more powerful in motivating people. Our second chapter addresses specific ideas on how to create both the threats and the opportunities to move an organization toward Six Sigma.

In Chapter 3, we focus on resistance. Resistance to Six Sigma is to be expected, even among the most productive of current employees. We discuss four major types of resistance, the underlying issues behind each type of resistance, and, most importantly, how to overcome these resistances.

Chapter 4 is devoted to how an organization can shape a Six Sigma Vision unique to their specific situation. The Six Sigma Vision is not just a mission statement. In addition to what a Six Sigma organization looks like, we address what the mindset of a Six Sigma organization looks like and finish this chapter examining the new behaviors of employees in a Six Sigma organization.

In Chapter 5, we address a host of issues dealing with acquiring greater Six Sigma acceptance. We discuss the importance of creating the internal resources for Six Sigma to thrive in your organization. Specifically we talk about the core competencies for a Quality Leader, your internal consultants, and trainers. We reveal the training secrets of the highest rated General Electric consultant, from what should be included in your training to how to conduct the training.

Additionally, in Chapter 5, we discuss how to create a reward and recognition program for both your Six Sigma professionals and the general employee population as a whole. Finally, we talk about the importance of communication in creating and sustaining acceptance to Six Sigma.

A hallmark of Six Sigma culture is measurement. In Chapter 6, we discuss the importance of measuring Six Sigma acceptance. We share a unique model we use with our clients that will assist your organization specifically determine how well your overall Six Sigma implementation effort is currently performing. From this evaluation, you can then develop a specific corrective action plan whether your needs are more on the technical side of Six Sigma implementation or on the cultural side of the implementation equation.

Since Six Sigma is first and foremost a management philosophy, Chapter 7 is devoted to specific suggestions on how to increase your Six Sigma management skills. In addition, we highlight several Six Sigma leaders and address what about them make them Six Sigma leaders.

In our final chapter, as we did in *The Six Sigma Revolution*, we discuss 10 different mistakes organizations make in their conscientious effort to gain greater acceptance to Six Sigma so you don't have to make the same mistakes others have.

Making Six Sigma Last: Managing the Balance Between Cultural and Technical Change is a critical read in any organization's effort at obtaining the results than Six Sigma can produce.

GEORGE ECKES

Acknowledgments

My deepest thanks to the staff of John Wiley and Sons for publishing my second book on Six Sigma. To Lisa Swayne, my book agent, who knows when to encourage and when to suggest change. To the staff of Publications Development Company for their Six Sigma editing. I am sure by our third book we will be seamless. To Matthew Holt, my John Wiley editor who knows more about Six Sigma than he probably cares to know.

For the friendship, loyalty, and wisdom of Dr. Susan Ayarbe. You are, and always will be, my closest friend. To my Uncle Joseph Della Malva, thank you for your love, inspiration, and connection to my dear mother. To Joe and Temo for being Six Sigma sons. To Dave Schulenberg, for your friendship, loyalty, and baseball knowledge. To Mike Multer for making the fall worthwhile. For my father, who shows change can happen at any age. Finally to my brother Mike, may you take the Lake Tahoe fishing trip you so richly deserve.

To Joseph L. Ayarbe, Susan Ayarbe, Elizabeth Campbell, Tiffany A. Davis, Gary E. Finch, Christina Pia Lomax, Evelyn R. Rie, and Roderick Smith for suggestions toward making this a better book.

G.E.

Contents

Chapter 1

Six Sigma Acceptance

The Ignored Element in Implementation

"You can choose not to change, but you can't do it here."

—Jack Welch

Within the last several years, Six Sigma has exploded onto the American scene as a prominent method of improving the effectiveness and efficiency of businesses. Companies like General Electric, AlliedSignal, and others have saved literally billions of dollars that have resulted in increased profitability and increased stock price. For example, since its adoption of Six Sigma in 1995, General Electric has saved more than 3 billion dollars. Jack Welch has said, "Six Sigma is the most important initiative we have ever undertaken."

Six Sigma is a management philosophy that attempts to improve customer satisfaction to near perfection. A Six Sigma company has little more than three bad customer experiences for every million opportunities. This level of near-perfect performance is a significant distance from where most organizations are today. It is estimated that most companies are at the two to three sigma performance level, which means that for every million customer contacts there are 308,000 to 66,800 defects.

Six Sigma moves an organization toward managing with facts and data. It is a management method that has customer satisfaction as its overriding philosophy. It achieves greater levels of customer satisfaction through focus and management of the processes of that organization.

To achieve greater customer satisfaction, there are three critical success factors: the strategic component, the tactical component, and the cultural component.

The strategy of Six Sigma is exclusively the domain of executive management. For Six Sigma to be more than just a cost savings initiative, management must create the infrastructure for improvement to occur. In my first Six Sigma book, *The Six Sigma Revolution: How General Electric and Others Turned Process Into Profits* (Wiley, 2000), I described in detail how management must create and manage the key processes of their organization so that Six Sigma activities move the strategic business objectives of the organization. I covered in detail how project teams apply the second major component of Six Sigma—the tactical component—so that processes begin to become more effective and efficient.

Making Six Sigma Last: Managing the Balance Between Cultural and Technical Change exclusively addresses the third and most important component of the critical success factors—the cultural component. It is the component most overlooked by organizations. It is the component that, if mastered by an organization, can drive quicker and more dramatic improvement in sigma performance. It is the component that most organizations ignore as they become preoccupied with the tactics of improvement. It is also the component that many Six Sigma consultants are unaware even exists.

■  $Q \times A = E$

This simple but powerful formula explains why an organization needs as much focus on the third component of the Six Sigma initiative as they do on the first two. The Q, *Quality*, in this formula refers to the strategic and tactical elements of the Six Sigma initiative. The A stands for the cultural *acceptance* of the strategic and tactical elements of Six Sigma. The E refers to the extent that a company achieves Six Sigma as a technical measure of performance.

The formula is multiplicative. Think of assigning a number between 1 and 10 for how well an organization is doing the Q of Six Sigma. Pick up any book on Six Sigma and the focus will be on Q. Even mature organizations would rate their performance as an 8 or 9. Then assign a number for how well the company is culturally accepting the Q. In most cases, asking this question provokes puzzled looks. Often management has done little, if anything, to manage the acceptance of Q in their organization. If this number is a 1 or 2, multiplying the two higher numbers gives 18.

$$9 \times 2 = 18$$

Is 18 a good number? If a perfect score is 100, what would you consider a passing score? I get the same answer that I do when I ask my two boys, Joe and Temo, what they would consider a passing score. To get an A in school, they would expect a 90 or better, a B would be scored as an 80 or better, a C would mean that the two numbers multiplied together would register a 70, and a mere passing grade would mean that the multiplied numbers would have to register at least a 60.

In this light, a score of 18 means the organization is not seeing the kinds of results typically associated with a Six Sigma initiative. Since in recent years management has invested significant costs and personal reputations on Six Sigma, there is usually a call to "re-double" the Six Sigma effort. What does this re-doubling of efforts look like? Obviously, the effort must be focused on cultural acceptance. In reality, if you don't know what elements increase cultural acceptance (and most companies don't), the re-doubling of efforts is spent on the Q. There is probably not much juice left in that fruit. So, after significant effort and investment, the organization moves from a 9 to a 9.5. Evaluating the re-doubling of efforts using our $Q \times A$ formula results in:

$$9.5 \times 2 = 19$$

The organization may start to question whether Six Sigma is for them. The company may give up the effort and return to their old ineffective and inefficient management methods.

Making Six Sigma Last is devoted to the many concepts, tools, and techniques that drive the second number in the $Q \times A = E$ formula. These concepts and tools are simple and direct. Compared to the statistical rigor and complexity of some of the Q tools, they may even seem elementary. However, a good consulting friend, Pam Dennis of Destra Consulting, said it best when she stated, "Implementing the hard tools of Six Sigma is easy, implementing the easy tools is hard."

What Pam meant is that the appearance of Six Sigma Q tools like a designed experiment or capability analysis may appear hard but after some teaching, they are relatively easy to implement. Those tools are applied to a process. Getting an organization to culturally accept change sounds easy, but deals first and foremost with human nature. Dealing with the human psyche is a complex endeavor. Thus, while the tools I will teach you in this book may seem relatively easy, you will not be applying them to processes, but to people. As such, the level of complexity rises exponentially.

The good news is that many organizations have gone before you. This aspect of Six Sigma has been taught successfully in statistical training of organizations worldwide for more than 20 years. Before I was a Six Sigma consultant, I trained and practiced as a psychologist. I am still licensed as a psychologist so I bring both training and experience to the $Q \times A = E$ equation.

Learning the tools in *Making Six Sigma Last* will be relatively easy. Becoming good at using them will take practice. There are six major areas to improve your A or acceptance number in the $Q \times A = E$ equation. This book will show you how to:

1. Create the need for Six Sigma.
2. Shape a vision of Six Sigma so that employees understand the desired results and new behaviors of a Six Sigma organization.
3. Mobilize commitment to Six Sigma and overcome resistance.
4. Change your systems and structures to support the new Six Sigma culture.
5. Measure Six Sigma cultural acceptance.
6. Develop Six Sigma leadership.

When teaching Six Sigma cultural leadership, I start by dividing my class into two groups. In the first group, I ask each individual to think of some change they have either played a part in, or been subjected to, that was highly successful. It can be a personal change or some professional change. I tell them not to talk about the specifics of the change but to keep their change in mind and then answer the following question:

What were the factors that contributed to making the change you are thinking of successful?

I tell the second group to think of either a personal or professional change they were a part of that was an unmitigated failure. This group usually has an easier time coming up with their personal examples. I then tell them to answer the following question:

What were the factors that contributed to making the change you are thinking of unsuccessful?

Over the course of the next 20 minutes of the exercise, the two groups brainstorm the factors without revealing their specific change. The two groups develop a list that is usually 10 to 12 items long. Then I tell them to narrow their list down to the most vital items that contributed to either the success or failure of the change they were thinking about. In the many years since I have started doing this exercise, I have collected data on the results. First, since they had the more difficult assignment, I ask the team that was thinking of the successful change for the criteria that made their change successful. Below is listed the most frequently provided reasons why a change was successful and the approximate percentage of time it has been mentioned as a reason why the change was successful:

Strong leadership	78%
The need for the change was communicated	59%
Clear and motivating goals and objectives	56%
Resistance was managed	44%
The culture was modified to encourage change	38%

It's now time for the second team to report on the criteria that contributed to unsuccessful change. The data for the group for unsuccessful change looks as follows:

Lack of clear goals	87%
The need for the change was never understood	79%
No or poor leadership	46%
Those against the change were allowed to win	40%
No incentives to change	32%

When comparing the two lists, it is obvious that patterns exist. In the multitude of times I have done this exercise, it is truly amazing to see over and over again the same reasons why a change has been successful and the same opposite set of reasons why it failed.

It became obvious that these patterns of simple but effective criteria could be built into a model. When that model is applied to Six Sigma, it could dramatically increase the potential for an organization to embrace not only Six Sigma as a management method that would result in everyone in the company practicing never-ending improvement, but actually be able to achieve Six Sigma as a technical measure of performance.

From my days as a psychologist, I was painfully aware that change, even positive change, is resisted. After several years as an in-patient therapist, I spent time in out-patient work doing a combination of individual, family, and marriage therapy. Doing marriage therapy as a single person was quite an education. It probably contributed to me waiting to walk down the aisle until I was in my thirties.

In the case of marriage therapy, my patience was always tested. More times than not, one spouse would want to work on the marriage while the other was oblivious to the need to change the conditions of the marriage. In case after case, one party was being abused either verbally, emotionally, physically, or in some rare cases all three. What amazed me was that in these cases the victim did not see change—divorce—as freedom from abuse. Instead, they saw change—divorce—as loss.

For the longest time I struggled with how someone in such a miserable existence could not see the opportunities that awaited a life free from pain. I then remembered the work of D. Chris Anderson at my beloved alma mater, the University of Notre Dame. While a junior in South Bend, I took several classes from who was to be my favorite professor. Dr. Anderson taught a variety of courses and did research on experimental psychology. His research showed change to be an exceedingly difficult choice for rats and for people.

I remember a study he did where a rat traversed the path of a gridded runway and we would measure the rat's travel time down the grid.

During certain periods of hunger, the rat would expediently traverse the grid. Then Dr. Anderson electrified the grid and exposed the hungry rat to the sight of his food at the end of the runway. As the rat entered the gridded runway, a shock, not such a significant voltage to cause death but to cause projectile defecation, ensued. Of course, this was not a pleasant experience for the rat (nor for those of us who had to clean up after the rat).

What Dr. Anderson then showed was a learning experience that has stayed with me for years. Trial after trial, the gridded runway leading to the rat's food was opened. Time and again, the rat just stayed in his cage. Even when the rat began to experience more advanced signs of malnutrition, and he would have his cage opened so he could visualize the food he so desperately needed for survival, he remained almost physically paralyzed.

Years later doing marriage counseling I thought of Dr. Anderson's experiments and the relationship those experiments had to real life. I came across an exercise I use to this day that highlights the same concepts I learned as a junior at Notre Dame.

I ask everyone in my seminar to stand and find a partner. If there are an odd number of seminar participants in the room I ask the odd person out to act as my assistant in the exercise. The rest of the participants are asked to face their partner. I tell each pair of participants to study their partner carefully for 30 seconds.

I then instruct each pair of individuals to turn back to back. I then slowly give them the instructions for Round 1 of the change exercise. I tell them to change three things about their physical appearance. I further tell them there is but one rule: they cannot create a hostile work environment.

During the following minute, the participants almost universally start doing the same thing, removing clothing. First, a pair of shoes are removed. Then a tie is loosened, or a belt removed, and a woman's earrings are taken off.

Nervous laughter pervades the room. In the event of an odd number of people in the room, my assistant is wandering about, gathering comments to be used in the debriefing of the exercise. I then instruct the participants to turn back to back again. I tell them that Round 2 is ready to begin. I instruct everyone to change five *additional* things about their physical appearance without changing any of the first three things.

No sooner have I provided these instructions when I and my assistant start hearing comments like:

➤ "I don't have any more clothes to take off."

➤ "I can't change anything more about myself."

➤ "This is ridiculous."

As they utter these comments, they continue to make changes. Again, I state the one rule of not creating a hostile work environment. In the years I have done this exercise, despite the nervous laughter and resistant comments, everyone has followed the instructions. After a minute, the participants are told to turn around and find the five additional things their partner changed.

After a few minutes, I then ask them to turn around for Round 3. As you might expect, the protest is both uniform and vocal. When I ask if the participants want to go a third round, the response is a virtually uniform "No."

As soon as I tell the participants to take a seat so we can talk about the exercise they quickly "re-dress." I ask them their reaction to the exercise. The comments are, for the most part, negative. I then ask them to collect data on the two rounds that they completed. By the end of the second round, they would have changed eight things about themselves. I instruct them to put their eight changes into three categories: changes they made where they *took something off,* changes that would be considered *neutral* (e.g., taking a watch from one hand and putting it on the other hand), and finally, *additions* they made to change their appearance.

In the years I have done this exercise, the statistics are:

Subtractions	70%
Neutral	25%
Additions	5%

Whether due to some previous negative experience with change or other explanations we will cover in later chapters, virtually everyone associates change with *loss* or *subtraction*. In one case during the debrief a participant said change is worse than seeing it as loss or subtraction, saying it felt more like division.

During the debriefing I note that there is even a biological explanation for the resistance to change. I ask my class to think of an individual in need of a heart transplant because their heart is diseased. What is the first thing that happens when a new, thriving heart is placed in the chest cavity of someone who would otherwise die? The heart is rejected, clear evidence of the biological resistance to change.

■ HOW THIS BOOK IS ORGANIZED

In the coming chapters we will address specific elements to soften the natural or acquired resistance to change. We will address how to systematically improve the chances of your Six Sigma effort being successful. For most organizations, Six Sigma introduces far more substantial change than most people realize at the onset of Six Sigma implementation.

Using the data from the exercise I use in my class about successful and unsuccessful change initiatives, it becomes apparent what is needed to drive successful change in general and successful Six Sigma specifically. While the journey toward successful change is not a linear path, the data shown earlier in the chapter does reveal key elements for successful change. Some of these elements come before others. In the following chapters, we address some of the elements that will drive improvement in the *A* part of the $Q \times A = E$ equation.

For successful change, the *need for change was communicated.* In the unsuccessful change group, the *need for change was never understood.* Thus, our second chapter addresses establishing the need for Six Sigma. In addition to learning how to create the need for Six Sigma, you will learn how to separate real from perceived reasons for Six Sigma to be the management approach adopted by your organization.

Forty percent of the unsuccessful group responded that *Those Against the Change Were Allowed to Win.* In the successful group, *Resistance Was Managed.* In Chapter 3, we address perhaps the most important of the elements that will move the *A* in the $Q \times A$ equation. Virtually any change initiative meets with resistance. This resistance will be compounded in a Six Sigma initiative where the amount of initial work can be daunting. Chapter 3 introduces you to how to conduct analysis on how significant the resistance to your Six Sigma initiative is, how to diagnose the four major types of resistance to a Six Sigma initiative, and the major strategies to combat them.

In Chapter 4, we address how to create Six Sigma goals that are not only clear, but more importantly, motivate those affected in an organization. We learn that Six Sigma cannot simply be a set of business or process improvement objectives. In addition to these Q metrics, there must also be a set of different behaviors in a Six Sigma organization. These behaviors must be motivating if Six Sigma is to be more than a fad in your organization.

I have had the good fortune to work for a variety of organizations that have solid reputations for Six Sigma implementation. During the 1980s I worked with several Motorola suppliers in their efforts to implement Six Sigma. In the 1990s I worked with over 20 of GE Capital's 30 businesses in their efforts at implementing Six Sigma. Several of these businesses did an outstanding job of implementation. In each case of successful Six Sigma implementation, the culture of the business embraced Six Sigma. In large measure, the management changed how business was conducted. At General Electric they call this changing the "systems and structures" of the business. Those that did well with changing the way they hired and developed their employees with Six Sigma in mind went a long way toward insurance that Six Sigma was successful. In addition, how management recognizes and rewards Six Sigma behaviors is crucial to its ultimate success. In Chapter 5, we devote our efforts to explaining in detail how to change the culture to make Six Sigma work.

In Chapter 5, you will also learn some of the training secrets of Eckes and Associates, Inc. Rated the most effective consulting group by GE Capital in 1998, we share our teaching secrets so that your Six Sigma training can be as effective as ours.

Six Sigma is, at its core, a management system based on decision making by fact and data. Measurement is a key to successful Six Sigma Q. The main theme of Chapter 6 is the measurement of the A of a Six Sigma initiative. In this chapter we provide suggestions on how to measure the cultural acceptance of Six Sigma, an ongoing measure that is as important as any Q measure. Once these cultural measures are collected, what to do with the measures to improve the Six Sigma culture will be discussed. We review five case studies of Six Sigma initiatives and discuss why they were either successful or unsuccessful.

In both the successful and unsuccessful change groups, we heard repeatedly that strong leadership (or the lack of it) was the critical element in the success of the change. No truer words were spoken. I have seen motivated individuals within an organization that desperately desired Six Sigma fail without the proper leadership. As Six Sigma is a management philosophy, how to gauge how well the business executive is leading Six Sigma is addressed in Chapter 7. How to improve Six Sigma leadership is covered and the chapter ends with selected profiles of successful Six Sigma leaders. This chapter specifically addresses what an executive must do to lead an effective and efficient Six Sigma effort.

In Chapter 8, we look at pitfalls to avoid in improving the $Q \times A$ equation.

■ SUMMARY

The management philosophy known as Six Sigma has three critical success factors: the strategic components, the tactics, and most important, the cultural component.

This book's focus is on the cultural component. Often overlooked in the Six Sigma implementation plan is the fact that Six Sigma is a major change for most organizations and how they manage. Studies have shown that change is associated with loss and humans resist loss. When Six Sigma initiatives are implemented, resistance is common. Thus, a successful Six Sigma organization will spend as much time on creating acceptance to Six Sigma as they do on the technical elements.

While Six Sigma has many statistics and equations associated with it, perhaps the most important equation for a Six Sigma culture is $Q \times A = E$. This equation states that the *quality* of the technical elements of the change multiplied by *acceptance* of the technical elements of change equals the excellence of the results. In this context, Q refers to how well an organization implements the strategies and tactics of Six Sigma. These elements are covered in detail in my first book, *The Six Sigma Revolution*. The A or acceptance of Six Sigma is the total focus of this book, *Making Six Sigma Last*.

KEY LEARNINGS

➤ Six Sigma is a proven management philosophy that can dramatically improve productivity by improving the effectiveness and efficiency of any organization.

➤ There are three components of Six Sigma: the strategic, the tactical, and the cultural.

➤ Most books on Six Sigma cover only the tactical aspects. *The Six Sigma Revolution* covered both the strategic and the tactical.

➤ This book, *Making Six Sigma Last*, exclusively addresses the last of the three concepts, the cultural acceptance of Six Sigma within your organization.

➤ When we refer to the cultural acceptance of Six Sigma, we will use the formula, $Q \times A = E$ which stands for the quality of your technical and strategic Six Sigma activities multiplied by the cultural acceptance equals the excellence of your Six Sigma results.

➤ The universal reaction to the word change is loss or subtraction.

(continued)

(Continued)

► In study after study of both successful and unsuccessful Six Sigma implementation several universal truths abound. First, the need for Six Sigma must be established.

► Second, that resistance to Six Sigma is normal and to be expected.

► Third, a vision of Six Sigma that incorporates the results, mindsets, and new behaviors of a Six Sigma organization must be established.

► Fourth, the systems and structures of an organization must be changed to reflect the new Six Sigma culture. Namely, how an organization hires with Six Sigma in mind, how an organization develops its employees with Six Sigma in mind, how it rewards and recognizes Six Sigma performance, and how its management communicates Six Sigma are vital to the cultural acceptance of Six Sigma.

► Fifth, to be successful with Six Sigma, measurement of the acceptance of Six Sigma is as important as measurement of the processes and defects of the organization.

► Sixth, Six Sigma will fail in any organization if leadership supporting Six Sigma is absent.

Chapter 2

Creating the Nee~~d~~
Six Sigma Culture

For Six Sigma to thrive in an organization, the need for Six Sigma must be established. Chapter 2 covers the two major ways in which people are motivated to see Six Sigma as the method that organizations need to adopt. The first method for people to be motivated to change is when they are confronted with real or perceived *threat*. The other way people are motivated to change is through real or perceived *opportunity*.

In this chapter we examine the tools used to capture both the threats and opportunities that an organization faces that would lead them to pursue Six Sigma implementation.

This chapter provides you with tried and proven threats to the status quo that have led many organizations to recognize the need for a change in how they manage their business toward Six Sigma. In addition to these threats, which are more likely to provide short-term motivation toward Six Sigma, the longer term opportunities that exist for an organization to pursue Six Sigma will be addressed.

finally, methods to communicate these threats and opportunities are reviewed so that the message received by each individual in the organization is personalized.

■ CREATING A NEED FOR CHANGE—
THE BILLY MARTIN STORY

Anyone who attends one of my seminars knows how much I love sports of all types, but especially baseball. I ask questions of my seminar participants and if you respond correctly you are far more likely to hear me say "Upper Deck Shot" (i.e., a home run answer) than you are to hear me say "Great answer." It should then come as no surprise that I use an extended baseball story to tell how one manager created the need for change.

My mother used to take my brother and me to Yankee Stadium. There we were caught up in the excitement of the 1960's Yankees, from Mickey Mantle to Roger Maris to lesser stars like Joe Pepitone and Elston Howard. Those years made me a life-long Yankee fan. I began to study the history of the Yankees and soon knew more than many ardent fans. One player I took an interest in was Billy Martin, one of Mickey Mantle's best friends. Billy Martin was the Yankee second baseman in the 1950s. He was not blessed with natural talent, yet he exceeded all expectations. He was fiery, not afraid to battle in either a figurative or literal fashion. He was also a student of the game and it soon became apparent that his baseball future was as a manager.

His first break came when the Minnesota Twins hired him in 1969. The Twins had lost their championship-caliber skills from years past and were playing poorly in 1968. Within one year Billy Martin had them winning the West Division before losing to the Baltimore Orioles in the playoffs.

Then his fiery temper cost him his job when he got into a fistfight with one of his pitchers, Dave Boswell.

At that time I lived in Michigan and had transferred my allegiance to the Detroit Tigers. The Tigers had lost many of the players that had them winning the 1968 World Series against the St. Louis Cardinals, coming back from a 3 game to 1 deficit. Then, early in the 1970s, the Tigers hired Billy and he led them to the division series within one year of hiring. Once again, he disturbed management and was fired.

In late 1973 the Texas Rangers took a flyer on Billy. Once again, as he did in Minnesota and Detroit, he took a substandard team who had lost more games than they had won in the previous year and led them to within five games of the division title. And as he did in Minnesota and Detroit, he left the Texas job when he encountered personality difficulties.

The soap opera that began in the late 1970s when Yankee owner George Steinbrenner first hired Billy to lead his beloved Yankees followed a similar pattern. Billy Martin was hired (and ultimately fired) a total of five times by George. During each term at the helm for the Bronx Bombers, he took a team that was struggling, turned them around and then they would tank, resulting in Billy being fired.

Billy Martin would probably have come back for the Yankees or some other team in trouble, in need of a quick turnaround artist. He was one who would take a troubled organization and get quick, though nonsustaining results. But on Christmas morning 1994 Billy Martin drove his pickup truck off the road and died.

In the early 1980s, I was fortunate to be trained in part by W. Edwards Deming, the noted quality expert who helped revolutionize Japan's economy after World War II. One of the things he taught me was never to make a decision based on one data point. In the Billy Martin story we have a clear pattern of behavior. He would take a struggling organization, quickly turn them around, only to have them return to their original poor performance in the second or third year of his management.

It is clear from studying Billy Martin's management style that he created a clear need for change in the organization who hired him. Of particular importance to note is that he would improve performance with the same personnel who the year before were substandard in the win column. Billy Martin's management style created a need for change through one major method: Fear. This fear was created by threats, either real or implied.

Threats are one of the two major ways to create a need for change. Threats, either real or perceived, motivate behavior. If I threaten to fire you if you don't get me a cup of coffee, it is clear how I create a need for you to change your behavior. However, whether it be the management style of Billy Martin or threatening to fire you to motivate the change of getting me a cup of coffee, creating a need for change based on threats typically is short lived.

A business example may prove illustrative. In 1984 I worked for a company called Storage Technology Corporation (StorageTek), responsible for creating a supplier improvement program. At the time, incoming reject rates were measured in double-digit percentages. It became my job to visit suppliers worldwide to have them practice the principles of Six Sigma so that their incoming materials could be shipped directly to stock or to the manufacturing line. Six months to the day I began working at StorageTek I was visiting a printed circuit board manufacturer outside of Boston. During the lunch break I was notified that StorageTek had just become the sixth largest company in U.S. history to file for Chapter 11 bankruptcy protection.

My first reaction was to wonder whether my airplane ticket was still valid for my return trip to Denver. Upon my return to the Mile High City, I was amazed at the short-term effect this bankruptcy filing had on the organization's interest in quality improvement. Like the man who dramatically changes his diet, stops smoking, and begins an exercise program, StorageTek suddenly showed a significant interest in my work with suppliers. Less than two months later the company was but one bankruptcy decision away from Chapter 7 liquidation.

By any account, this was a real and dramatic threat to the organization. I was asked to participate in several conferences to expedite the quality effort. Suppliers who, after the filing had suddenly become creditors to StorageTek began asking for my services.

Within months, the status quo returned. What I had believed was the need for change had suddenly come and gone. Like the man with the heart attack who goes back to eating donuts, StorageTek and their suppliers returned to the methods that in part had driven them to Chapter 11 in the first place. Eventually, StorageTek came out of Chapter 11 to become a thriving organization, but I learned a valuable lesson about threats motivating behavior.

What I learned from this experience is that threats tend to be good, short-term motivators of change. To create and sustain the need for change in the long-term, there must be more than just threats. On the flip side of the threat coin are the opportunities that help to drive the longer term need for change.

Several years ago I was presenting a seminar in Connecticut. On my drive to the convention center, I suddenly ran into this massive traffic jam in the middle of Stamford, Connecticut. Along the sidewalks were hoards of people in long lines. Down each side street were buses that had transported these people into town. When I got to the convention center, I inquired of several people what was going on. It turns out that Connecticut was one of the few states offering "PowerBall," a high-powered lottery giving away millions of dollars through picking a series of numbers. Each day the winning number eluded the thousands that would plunk down their dollar to pick a series of numbers that would result in their winning 80 million dollars. Finally after a few weeks, those people in bordering states would hire buses to drive them to the participating states like Nebraska and Connecticut where they would proceed to wait in lines at convenience stores for hours on end. In my case, at 7:00 in the morning, lines had been formed before daybreak by people who boarded buses in the middle of the night to make the trek to Connecticut.

What created this need for change in the daily habits of thousands of people who ordinarily would be in bed at that time of day? The *opportunity* to win millions.

■ THE THREATS AND OPPORTUNITIES OF SIX SIGMA

To increase the Cultural Acceptance in the $Q \times A$ formula we discussed in Chapter 1, I advise clients to create both the threats and opportunities that help create the need for Six Sigma in their organizations. There is not one perfect set of threats and opportunities for every organization. Some threats and some opportunities are better for some organizations than others. The exercise that follows is a way for any organization to create their unique set of threats and opportunities.

First, separate the executive team randomly into two groups. In one corner of the room, have a flip chart with the following question:

*What will happen to [the organization's name] if we suc-
cessfully implement Six Sigma?*

One group is assigned to answer this question. The other
executive subgroup moves to another corner of the room
where a flip chart has the following question:

*What will happen to [the organization's name] if we
don't successfully implement Six Sigma?*

I tell them to use a tool called an *affinity diagram* to complete their work. In front of each executive subgroup is a pile
of sticky notes and flip chart pens. I instruct each participant
to write answers to the question on sticky notes and stick
them on the wall. Once that assignment is complete, while I
take one of the executive subgroups, my assistant takes the
other. Each of us read each note from our respective subgroups. As we read each note, we instruct the participants to
say nothing if they understand what is read. We make a special point to instruct the group not to comment on the note
unless they don't *understand* what is written. If they vehe-
mently disagree with what is written they should remain
silent. This last instruction can be particularly difficult with
hard-driving executives who have an opinion on everything.
However, we emphasize that this tool is an example of the
rigor and discipline that Six Sigma provides an organization.

As my associate and I clarify each note, we place identical notes on top of one another. We group similar notes together. Once the notes have been reviewed, duplicates
matched, and grouped, each grouping is reviewed to determine a category name.

One group's brainstorming to "What will happen to
_____ if we successfully implement Six Sigma?"
resulted in the following groups of notes:

1. Increase our profits/increase market share/sustain current customer base.

2. Be seen as a leader in our field/prominence as a world-class organization.

3. Increase employee satisfaction/increase employee retention.

4. Greater organizational efficiency/greater organizational effectiveness.

For the first set of ideas (Increase our profits/increase market share/sustain current customer base), I ask the executive subgroup to come up with a category name. They propose *Improved Profitability*. For the next set of ideas (Be seen as a leader in our field/prominence as a world-class organization), the executive subgroup generates the category name *Greater World-Class Performance*. For the third group of ideas (increased employee satisfaction/increased employee retention), the category name generated was *Increased Employee Development*. Last, for the group of ideas of greater organization efficiency/greater organizational effectiveness, the category my subgroup of executives chose was *Greater Productivity*.

While I was working with this group, my associate was doing the exact same thing with the other executive subgroup. When her work was complete, the group that had brainstormed what would happen to the organization if they did not successfully implement Six Sigma had come up with the following list of categories:

1. Reduced customer base.

2. Increased employee frustration.

3. Competitors improving through use of Six Sigma.

4. Layoffs.

5. Chapter 11 (bankruptcy filing).

My associate and I bring both subgroups back together. Each group is expected to "pitch" or sell to the other group their brainstormed reasons to see which of the reasons (if any) work for their organization. Usually, the competitive juices of the executive team flow. They find themselves trying to convince the other group of the reasons for Six Sigma to exist in their organization. In this example, I give 10 to 15 minutes for each group to convince the other of their reasons. For any reason the other group accepts, I then ask if that reason would occur within the next 12 months (considered the short term) or beyond 12 months (considered long term). From the exercise, we create a matrix of the accepted threats and opportunities:

Short-Term Threats	**Short-Term Opportunities**
➤ Competitors improving through use of Six Sigma ➤ Increased employee frustration	
➤ Reduced customer base	➤ Improved profitability ➤ Greater productivity ➤ Increased employee development
Long-Term Threats	**Long-Term Opportunities**

The good news is that each group convinced the other group of *some* of the other groups reasons. The bad news is that each group failed to convince the other group of *all* their proposed reasons. Let's find out why.

➤ Eckesism 201 — If You Can't Prove It, Don't Use It

In my seminars, I provide clichés that my clients can use to guide them through their Six Sigma journey. Eckesism #1 I created when I received feedback from a seminar participant that I didn't agree with: "Feedback is a gift, some gifts can be returned."

While I don't have 201 Eckesisms, I do believe in this one strongly. A big mistake companies make, particularly with threats, is to come up with scary reasons that cannot be substantiated. Let's examine each of the threats that the other executive subgroup did not agree with:

Layoffs

The threat team claimed that layoffs would occur if the organization did not implement Six Sigma. This would normally be a powerful threat to create the need for a Six Sigma initiative if it could be proven. But in this organization, this was not the case. Using a threat that sounds good but cannot be proven calls into question the threats that are real. If this was a true threat for your organization and can be substantiated, by all means use it. When I was at StorageTek at the time of the Chapter 11 filing, I could have used this short-term threat and I could prove it. Within a week of the Chapter 11 filing, layoffs began. On each Friday, the lobby of each of the eight buildings would fill with cardboard boxes. By the end of the day, those who would be laid off would be called into their manager's office and asked to clean out their cubicle. On Friday afternoons, the Boulder, Colorado, bars would fill up with the "survivors" who were not called in to their manager's office, talking about whether they would be called in to the manager's office next Friday.

At the time, if I had used as a short-term threat that failure to implement Six Sigma at StorageTek would have resulted in greater layoffs, I would have had the proof. However, in the executive example just cited, the threat of layoffs was not in any way certain and would have resulted in the "Boy-Who-Cried-Wolf" syndrome.

Remember that story? A shepherd's child who was responsible for tending a flock of sheep cried wolf. The townspeople ran and, alas, there was no wolf. He did it again, with the concerned townspeople running to assist the little boy. Again, no wolf. Then a third and final time, the boy actually does see a wolf, cries for assistance from the townspeople, but this time they think it's a false alarm and the sheep are slaughtered.

This story should be kept in mind when a team is thinking of the threats that would create the need for Six Sigma in their organization.

Chapter 11 (Bankruptcy filing)

The same rationale would apply here as it did for the lay-off issue. This was an organization with several financial pressures that led them to consider a Six Sigma initiative, but in no case were they close to this financially dramatic step. This leads us to another Eckesism that should be considered when creating the threats (or opportunities for that matter) in creating the need for Six Sigma in an organization.

➤ Eckesism 202—Less Is More When It Comes to Threats and Opportunities

Each time I do this exercise with clients they tend to think more is better. In organizations I have worked with that have done a good job on creating the need for Six Sigma, the documented needs do not constitute a long laundry list. Instead, there are a few potent reasons that people in the organization can buy in to. Yet, in most organizations there is the belief that if they bombard the employee with a multitude of reasons, they will win their battle by wearing down the audience. Or, to put it another way, if we throw enough mud at the wall, something will stick. This should not be the case when it comes to creating the need. Instead, create a small list of both threats and opportunities and create the argument for them to work in your organization that is undisputed.

■ DOCUMENT YOUR THREATS AND OPPORTUNITIES

Once the team has agreed on the threats and opportunities that exist for their organization to adopt Six Sigma, it is important to have documentation for the respective threat or opportunity. It will come as no surprise to those who have tried to convince others of the need for Six Sigma that proof is needed for any given threat or opportunity. Let's examine those proofs that were convincing in our exercise.

The first short-term threat that was accepted was: *Competitors improving through use of Six Sigma.* This example comes from a client who was in competition with both GE Capital and AlliedSignal. At the beginning of the 1990s, this client was considered on a par with both GE and Allied-Signal. At the time of this exercise, they were considered a distant third as a competitor using profitability, growth, and market research among common customers.

The second short-term threat that was accepted was *Increased employee frustration.* The data that documented that employees were frustrated came from two sources. First, an annual employee survey had shown gradual decreases in employee satisfaction. Second, employee turnover had steadily increased within our client's organization during the time that GE Capital and AlliedSignal had adopted a Six Sigma management philosophy.

The remaining threat that was considered documented was if this organization didn't adopt a Six Sigma initiative there would be attrition in their customer base. While this may appear a trickier element to document, the team was convinced when shown a series of customer contracts that had not been renewed in the last two years due to failure to meet minimum quality requirements. It was not a hard sell to claim that further avoidance of Six Sigma implementation was going to cost a current customer contract. The customer had a two-year contract requirement of a minimum incoming quality yield of 98 percent. Currently, the incoming yield was 91 percent and the long-term contract was to be voided if this organization did not increase the yield to the desired 98 percent within 18 months.

Opportunities must be documented in the same way as threats. *Improved profitability* is the easiest opportunity to document. A cursory review of literature shows how improving Six Sigma performance can improve the bottom line. In the first year of General Electric's Six Sigma effort, they spent millions and broke even. Within 5 years, they had saved literally billions. Lipper Analytical is on record as saying that 20 percent of General Electric's stock price was due to General Electric's *reputation for practicing Six Sigma*. The same documentation can be stated for increased productivity. For example, Pilkington Libbey Owens Ford slashed $20 million in operating expenses using Six Sigma. They reduced the scrap rate for an Isuzu window panel by 75 percent and reduced the cost of glass for an annualized savings of over $2.4 million in that process alone. The Navistar Truck Group is saving the company nearly $1 million a year. At Navistar, a Sky Rise Roof team is saving nearly $220,000 annually. There are a host of other companies increasing productivity in a similar manner.

The last opportunity was: *Increased employee development.* The documentation for this was again based on benchmarking organizations that had successfully implemented Six Sigma. General Electric has had significant improvement in employee satisfaction and, ultimately, employee development.

■ BALANCE IN THE MATRIX

I am often asked whether it is important to have balance within the four quadrants of the threat/opportunity matrix. Ideally, the answer is yes. However, I don't tell clients this because they tend to waste valuable time trying to "complete" the matrix. I always stress that an "imbalanced" yet persuasive set of threats and opportunities beats a less persuasive but balanced set of threats and opportunities. Typically, at a minimum, short-term threats and long-term opportunities should be evident on the threat/opportunity matrix.

■ STRATIFY YOUR MESSAGE TO THE STAKEHOLDER

When completing this exercise, both groups justifiably derive some satisfaction from "convincing" the other executive subgroup of their respective threats and opportunities. They are not finished, however. Once a threat or opportunity has been established, it must be streamlined to the audience being targeted. Streamlining the message to the targeted audience is based on knowing who the stakeholder is.

A stakeholder is not the same as a customer. A customer is the recipient of a product or service. A stakeholder is someone who is either affected by Six Sigma or necessary to implement Six Sigma.

Think of the first long-term opportunity that was accepted, *Improved profitability*. If the stakeholder was a manager in the bonus program, increased profitability might be communicated in terms of what percent of his or her bonus could be increased through Six Sigma implementation. At General Electric, Jack Welch talked about how 40 percent of a manager's bonus was linked to his or her participation in the Six Sigma initiative. Of course, in this context, the message to General Electric management could easily be construed to be a threat (i.e., "If you don't participate in Six Sigma your 40 percent bonus could be at risk"). Yet, if the stakeholder was a manager, greater profitability could be personalized in this manner.

If the stakeholder was an individual contributor, greater profitability could be translated into larger profit sharing in their 401(k) program, or gain sharing in project participation, or greater job security, or some combination of all of these.

Regardless of how the message is personalized, it is imperative that whatever threat or opportunity is generated be communicated in a personal way that affects the stakeholder targeted for creating the need.

■ MAKE YOUR OWN LIST

I have used an actual client's experience to show how one organization created their threats and opportunities to help create the need for Six Sigma. The concept of benchmarking is not applicable for this exercise. There is a significant psychological advantage to going through this exercise and creating threats and opportunities that are unique to your business. Don't assume that the reasons that help create the need for the organization referenced in our example will apply to your organization. In my years of doing this exercise for clients, I do see some similar patterns. But, even if your organization comes up with an identical list to that shown earlier, the process of getting there helps build the commitment that is a necessary requirement of building better buy-in for Six Sigma in your organization.

■ SUMMARY

It is recommended that an organization first and foremost create the need for change for Six Sigma. This chapter addressed the idea that the need for Six Sigma can be created through threats, real or perceived, and opportunities.

Threats are good at creating the need for Six Sigma in the short-term. We defined the short-term as a threat that would occur to the organization within the next 12 months. While threats can occur beyond 12 months (called long-term threats), most threats will be short-term in nature. While threats are important to jump-start the need for Six Sigma, opportunities sustain the need for Six Sigma. Opportunities that typically can be documented beyond 12 months tend to be long-term. Thus, a balance of threats and opportunities are required if the need for Six Sigma is to be established.

Many organizations make a common mistake in creating the need for Six Sigma by thinking that if they can create a long list of threats and opportunities at least some will work if not all. This approach to creating the need for Six Sigma is disastrous. Those who resist Six Sigma will focus on your weaker threats and opportunities and dilute the effect of your stronger arguments.

Even when an organization has created their threats and opportunities, they must streamline the message to the audience. In every organization there will be those individuals who are affected by Six Sigma or are needed to implement Six Sigma. These individuals are called *stakeholders* and we examined how a similar concept (increased profitability) should be modified depending on the audience.

Finally, this chapter used several of the threats and opportunities I have seen in practice. While factual, this chapter covered in pragmatic fashion how to create the threats and opportunities for any organization. We strongly recommend taking the methods covered in this chapter and creating your own threats and opportunities rather than just using the threats and opportunities mentioned in this chapter.

KEY LEARNINGS

➤ For Six Sigma to thrive in an organization, employees at all levels of the organization must see the need for Six Sigma.

➤ There are two major ways for the need for Six Sigma to be established in an organization. In one case, the threats, real or perceived, must be firmly established. The other way for the need for Six Sigma to be established in an organization is through the opportunities that await the Six Sigma organization.

➤ Threats motivate short-term behaviors. Opportunities motivate long-term behaviors.

➤ The threats and opportunities that create the need for Six Sigma vary from organization to organization.

(continued)

(Continued)

➤ Only use the best threats and opportunities. Don't be mistaken in the belief that a laundry list of threats and opportunities will create the need. More often than not, those that prefer not to see the need focus on your less persuasive threats and opportunities to justify ignoring the need for Six Sigma.

➤ Be ready to prove the threat or opportunity. Remember, if you can't prove it, don't use it.

➤ Streamline your message to your audience. Stakeholders need to have the threat or opportunity crafted in a way that makes sense for them.

Chapter

Overcoming Six Sigma Resistance

"You can't go the distance, with too much resistance."

—Billy Joel

In Chapter 1, we learned that change in any organization will uniformly be met with resistance. There are four major types of resistance and the type of resistance to Six Sigma must be properly diagnosed so that an effective strategy to overcome the resistance is created. In this chapter, the four types of resistance to Six Sigma are defined, the underlying issues of each type of resistance are discussed and, finally, strategies to overcome the resistance are reviewed. In over 80 percent of times, successful implementation of the strategies results in previous resistors becoming Champions of the Six Sigma initiative. What to do in those 20 percent of cases when the strategy fails will also be discussed.

■ RESISTANCE—THE UNIVERSAL REACTION TO CHANGE

In Chapter 1, I shared an exercise that showed that when a group of seminar participants are asked to change three to eight things about their physical appearance they immediately and consistently begin taking elements of their clothing off. During the debrief of the exercise, the participants learned that they saw a strong association between thinking of change with loss.

If it is human nature to associate the word change with loss, it may be expected that those presented with changing their culture through Six Sigma will resist the Six Sigma effort initially no matter how many benefits a Six Sigma culture will provide the organization.

Those who see the power of Six Sigma often do not understand those who don't immediately see Six Sigma in the same way. This makes the problem even more complex. This chapter is written for those who endorse Six Sigma as much as it is written for those who exhibit the patterns of resistance mentioned in this chapter.

There are four major steps to the successful mobilization of commitment to the Six Sigma initiative. They are:

1. Identification of the key stakeholders of the Six Sigma initiative.

2. Identification of the current level of support or resistance to the quality initiative by each key stakeholder.

3. Identification of where each key stakeholder must be in order for the initiative to be successful.

4. Development of strategies to move each stakeholder to the desired level of support to be successful.

➤ Identification of Key Stakeholders

Stakeholders are those affected by the Six Sigma initiative or those needed to implement Six Sigma. It is important to identify the key stakeholders—those stakeholders who have leverage or influence over other stakeholders. For example, if the Vice President of Sales and Marketing has the ability to influence other stakeholders in the Sales and Marketing function, he or she would be considered a key stakeholder.

➤ Identification of the Current Level of Support or Resistance to the Quality Initiative by Each Key Stakeholder

There are five possible positions for a key stakeholder to occupy. First, there are those who may currently be *making Six Sigma happen*. We will call this the strongly supportive group. Second, there may be stakeholders who are *helping Six Sigma happen*. We will call this the moderately supportive group. The third position is those who are *letting Six Sigma happen*. We will call this the neutral group. In each of these cases, depending on the importance of the key stakeholder, it is possible that Six Sigma could be successful.

The last two positions that a key stakeholder could occupy are those who are *moderately against having Six Sigma happen* and those who are *strongly against having Six Sigma happen*.

Each of these five positions can be operationally defined. Those who are *making Six Sigma happen* are not only doing what is asked of them but in addition to successfully taking their action items, they act as advocates to convince others of the importance of Six Sigma.

Those who are *helping Six Sigma happen* dutifully complete what is asked of them in terms of Six Sigma but do nothing more.

Those who *let Six Sigma happen* may passively comply to what is asked of them but most importantly they will let Six Sigma activity occur and not disturb its progress. In general, they don't have strong feelings one way or another toward managing with Six Sigma. To say that a person is neutral to

Six Sigma indicates they have been informed about Six Sigma and neither support or impede it. This category should not be used for those who have not been informed about Six Sigma.

Those who are described as *moderately against having Six Sigma happen* will explicitly not comply with what is asked of them relative to Six Sigma implementation.

Finally, those that are described as *strongly against having Six Sigma happen* will not only explicitly not comply with what is asked of them relative to Six Sigma implementation, but in addition will lobby against the Six Sigma initiative, actively trying to recruit other *terrorists* against the Six Sigma effort.

Categorizing the current level of commitment to Six Sigma should be done through a Stakeholder Analysis Chart (Table 3.1).

The Stakeholder Analysis Chart is filled out as to the current level and desired level of support for Six Sigma. Table 3.2 is the chart of a recent client who asked for a stakeholder analysis to be conducted.

In the preceding stakeholder analysis, a circle "O" represents where the stakeholder is *currently* relative to Six Sigma support. The "X" represents the targeted goal of where that particular stakeholder *needs to be* in order for Six Sigma to be successful within the organization. It is important to note several elements of the chart. First, not everyone has to be in the "Make It Happen" column. In fact, my experience indicates that successful Six Sigma initiatives need only two major functions in the "Make It Happen" column, Upper Management and Human Resources. The need for Upper Management to be in the last column is self-evident. And as we shall see in later chapters, the Human Resource function plays an important role in the implementation of many of the cultural elements of Six Sigma.

Key Stakeholder	Strongly Against Having Six Sigma Happen	Moderately Against Having Six Sigma Happen	Lets Six Sigma Happen	Helps Six Sigma Happen	Makes Six Sigma Happen
Vice President of Sales/Marketing					
Vice President of Manufacturing					
Executive Management					
Human Resource Management					
Finance Management					
Vice President of Quality					

Table 3.1 Stakeholder analysis chart.

A second benefit of the Stakeholder Analysis Chart is knowing that most stakeholders who are against Six Sigma are only moderately against it. While it should not surprise anyone when an organization finds a stakeholder strongly against, creating the Stakeholder Analysis Chart often shows things are not as bad as they initially may appear.

Key Stakeholder	Strongly Against Having Six Sigma Happen	Moderately Against Having Six Sigma Happen	Lets Six Sigma Happen	Helps Six Sigma Happen	Makes Six Sigma Happen
Vice President of Sales/Marketing		O-----------	-----------------------	-----------X	
Vice President of Manufacturing			O-------------------X		
Executive Management			O----------	-----------------------	----------X
Human Resource Management				O-------------------X	
Finance Management		O-------------------X			
Vice President of Quality				X--------------	----------O

Table 3.2 Example—Stakeholder analysis chart.

Third, it is more manageable when you know that there are those stakeholders who only need to let Six Sigma happen and the initiative will be successful. In the previous example, Finance Management is only moderately against. Our target position for them is the "Let It Happen" category.

The bad news in the example is no stakeholder group is where they need to be in order for the Six Sigma initiative to be successful. When movement is necessary from where a stakeholder may be today to where they need to be tomorrow, resistance may and will likely be encountered.

We now address the four major types of resistance, what are the underlying issues behind the resistance, and strategies to combat the resistance.

■ TECHNICAL RESISTANCE—THE MOST COMMON TYPE OF RESISTANCE

Ten years ago I could not operate a lap-top computer. Those who knew me at the time knew that I would disparage computers in a rather direct and sometimes profane way. At the time my thinking was that Power Point was a sharpened pencil. I was convinced of the inefficiency of computers, recalling a huge mistake I had made in front of the largest crowd I had ever given a speech to, using a computer.

The speech was at the Anaheim Convention Center and as the keynote speaker I was told that more than 900 people would hear my message. Knowing the importance of my message, I created a 35mm presentation and with the assistance of one of my associates used a computer to create a set of slides to accompany my speech.

I was impressed with the slide presentation and briefly thought that I had been childish about the power of computers, thinking that this new tool could perhaps make my presentations more powerful. On the day of my speech, I began in earnest speaking to the large crowd. Humor is a part of each of my presentations and soon the crowd responded to some of my funnier lines. Then as I clicked to my next slide, I began to hear a growing snickering among the participants that grew to loud laughter like I never had experienced before or since. Knowing I had not said anything remotely humorous, I turned around to see that the words "Pubic Sector" (Public Sector) had passed by the computer's spellchecker.

Being more embarrassed than I had ever felt before, I proceeded through the remainder of my speech but the audience didn't take me seriously after seeing my faux pas. My reaction to computers became stronger than ever. I never would have allowed such a mistake if I hadn't used a computer, I thought. I projected my lack of professionalism on the computer, not my deficiencies. At the time, I had convinced myself that computer spellcheckers would have prevented that type of mistake but I was wrong.

Talking with my wife on my arrival back in Denver, my resistance was stronger than ever. She politely suggested a computer class. I reluctantly agreed and signed up for a computer class at a local college.

Within the first few minutes of the computer class, I recognized the brilliance of the instructor. He was talented, animated, and clearly knew the subject. However, in the long run that may have been the problem. At the end of an eight-week class, I left with an even stronger resistance to computers.

After my Anaheim speech and the computer class, I could only be described as the most resistant person on the planet to computers. My resistance was not limited to me. I would actively talk to friends and associates, trying to convince them of the folly of computers, and trying to recruit them to my cause.

Of course my recruitment efforts were unsuccessful. However, it did make me feel better, albeit short-lived. After several efforts at recruitment that failed, I became a "covert terrorist," silent in my virulent resistance.

This story has a happy ending. Slowly and gradually, my resistance began to change. My two wonderful boys, Joe and

Temo, are very much like most boys their age—they are computer literate. They would share their happiness with playing computer games and how they could expedite their homework through use of the computer. They would inform me of the benefits of their use of the computer. In a non-threatening manner, they would educate me on how they were using the computer in a positive and rewarding way. Soon they began to involve me in some of their computer activities, both for school and for entertainment. Without my apparent conscious efforts, I began "logging on" and, within a much shorter time than I ever expected, I soon began responding to my own e-mail rather than delegating this responsibility to my wife. The crowning achievement was having my first book written exclusively on my computer.

This story highlights the most common type of resistance to change that applies to Six Sigma implementation: *That which is not understood is resisted.* In my case, I pride myself on my intelligence. The computer made me feel stupid. From this experience I began thinking how what I took for second nature in Six Sigma, must have made normally intelligent people feel toward Six Sigma like I felt toward the computer.

I soon realized that one type of resistance to Six Sigma was based on the underlying issue of Six Sigma making a person feel inept. I recalled the experiences I had with a General Electric employee who, to this day, I deeply respect for her myriad skills but someone who might have felt much like I did toward computers.

I first met this General Electric employee, an organizational development specialist, in 1997. If I have the reputation for being a Six Sigma expert, she clearly has the reputation for being an organizational development expert. Her training skills are exceptional, as well as her ability to read an audience. Therefore, it was natural for her to be chosen by GE Capital business to be a Six Sigma trainer. It was in this context we first met. From the beginning, she showed all the classic signs of technical resistance. Twenty minutes before we were in the measure phase of Six Sigma training, she complained to me about the subject in the hallway. Dutifully, she completed each and every assignment (accurately I might add), but her complaining to me was incessant. Having just had success-fully experienced the Involvement, Information, and Educa-tion approach practiced by my sons on me, I tried a similar approach on her technical resistance to Six Sigma calcula-tions.

The results were amazingly similar. I first provided infor-mal education by walking her through a series of process im-provement project baseline Six Sigma calculations that she was supervising. As I provided informal education, she even responded to a calculation by saying "Hey, that wasn't that tough."

Next, I provided her with the two ways to measure base-line Six Sigma, the discrete and continuous measures. Most people find the discrete method significantly easier than the continuous method. I simply asked her which of the two methods she thought was easier (Involvement), and her nat-ural intelligence took over, not only by indicating to me which of the methods she thought was easier, but then mak-ing the case for herself why the continuous method was probably a more accurate method, albeit more difficult.

Today, this individual is doing Six Sigma training for an organization where project teams repeatedly seek her out for Six Sigma consulting including the calculations. While she would never consider herself a statistician, she clearly has mastered the skills she once resisted.

It is critical to recognize that the underlying issue be-hind technical resistance is fear and that change often makes you feel inadequate or stupid. If the underlying issues are fear and feelings of inadequacy, formal training may ultimately cause more fear and feelings of inadequacy, resulting in greater resistance. This can especially be the case regarding Six Sigma.

Six Sigma is a methodology that relies on management with facts derived from data. Portions of successful Six Sigma initiatives are dependent on statistics. Many teachers of Six Sigma are trained statisticians. Trained statisticians sometimes are more interested in theory than application.

A recent client of mine had me do the training for the first wave of Six Sigma projects. After a successful completion of the first wave of training, they were interested in hiring me for a second wave of training. Due to other commitments, I declined and they hired a competitor. Within a few weeks, they told me the second wave training was a disaster. Instead of learning how to use the statistics to manage with facts and data, this competitor was teaching statistical theorems and algebra. Imagine having technical resistance to Six Sigma and sitting through a course being confused over nonrelevant material that increased your feelings of inadequacy. I soon freed up my calendar to assist this client finish the second wave of training (after my competitor was jettisoned), but found many of the class participants exhibiting classical signs of technical resistance.

What does technical resistance look like? As I took over this class midstream, I received more questions centered around relatively insignificant but highly detailed issues. I have come to the conclusion that those suffering technical resistance become overwhelmed with highly specific, detailed elements of Six Sigma tools and techniques. Their questions are very detailed, as if they need to be further confused to feed and validate their resistance. I call it the *Vein Theory*. Some people don't see the forest for the trees. At times those experiencing technical resistance are preoccupied with the veins on the leaf on the branch of a tree in a huge forest when they need to be focused on the forest.

My strategy to overcome this class' significant technical resistance was to focus on the higher level concepts, encourage their competence when shown and build on small successes so that slowly and eventually they felt less and less inadequate and Six Sigma no longer made them feel the way they did when they were being taught mathematical theorems instead of what Six Sigma is all about.

■ POLITICAL RESISTANCE

Years ago a large computer firm hired me to create a supplier improvement program for their suppliers worldwide. At the time their incoming reject rate was overwhelming. This meant that parts that went into making their computers were received at their incoming receiving dock and had to be inspected and sorted out before being sent on to their production lines for assembly.

Management of this computer client asked my firm to begin improving quality at the source. My associates were to visit key suppliers and begin improving product at the point of manufacturing rather than waiting for parts to be sorted once they arrived at the computer manufacturing areas.

For my associates to do their job, we needed to work closely with the receiving inspection department of my client, identifying the most important suppliers, the suppliers with the worst performance and so on. To do my job to implement Six Sigma within their supplier community, I needed the support of the receiving inspection department.

I won't soon forget the first day I spent with the Receiving Inspection Vice President. After an exchange of pleasantries at a management meeting, the Receiving Inspection Vice President called me into his office. No sooner was the door closed when he said:

I don't like you. I don't like what you are going to try to do. I hope your stay here is short and unpleasant and I plan to do everything in my power to prevent you from making any changes. We run a great operation and I will be damned if you or anyone else does anything to change that.

While it was hard not to react personally to this attack, I was fortunate to recognize one of the more direct examples of Political Resistance. Clearly this Vice President was not exhibiting Technical Resistance. He understood why I was there and what I was chartered to do with his suppliers. In fact, his clear understanding of Six Sigma helped propel his Political Resistance to the concept.

Political Resistance is that type of resistance that exists when the proposed change is seen as a threat to the status quo. Remember, the universal perception of change is loss or subtraction. This is also the underlying issue behind Political Resistance. Those exhibiting this resistance see the change as a loss. Sometimes the loss is perceived. Sometimes the loss is real. Our Receiving Inspection Vice President was in a situation where there was both real *and* perceived loss.

If the psychological reaction to change is perceiving it as loss and there are situations in which the loss is real, how can we ever mobilize the level of commitment needed by individuals exhibiting this type of resistance?

Actually, the odds are on our side. Informal data I have collected over the years has led me to the conclusion that of those who initially are either moderately or strongly resistant to change, 80 percent are changeable. The other way of looking at this is no matter what advice you follow in this book, about 20 percent of resistors are and always will be resistant to change.

In company after company where I have implemented Six Sigma, a small percentage immediately are drawn to my argument to become more effective and efficient. I call these people the "Champions of change." The middle groups of individuals who comprise most of the organization I call the "Silent Majority." These folks are neither for nor against Six Sigma at the beginning but will move in the general direction of where the organization moves, either positive motion toward Six Sigma or negative. Last is the general category of people in the organization who I affectionately call the "Terrorists" of the organization. My research tells me that approximately 80 percent of Terrorists are changeable based on following the advice in Chapter 3.

First, in the case of real loss, the change agent must be honest with the person showing resistance. If I had been smarter, I would have acknowledged to the Vice President of Receiving Inspection that if my firm was successful, ultimately there would be no need for Receiving Inspection. Being honest with a stakeholder is both critical and often ignored.

While it was true that Receiving Inspection would be eliminated as the company had historically practiced it, Supplier Assurance would thrive and grow. One of the people who reported to the Receiving Inspection Vice President, the Electrical Inspection Director, saw the *addition* that my consulting would bring to the organization. My consulting group began working with their suppliers with the assistance of the Electrical Inspection Director. These projects were mostly successful. The Electrical Inspection Director's prestige and power grew while the Receiving Inspection Vice President's stature diminished.

Ultimately, as we became successful, the Receiving Inspection Vice President left the company voluntarily. His position was eliminated. The position of Vice President of Supplier Assurance was created and filled by the Electrical Inspection Director. Therein lies the strategy to combat political resistance. While it is important to empathize with the real loss, it is vital to emphasize what is gained through the benefits of implementing Six Sigma. In this case, the Electrical Inspection Director saw that supporting our efforts at improving quality at the supplier's site would create greater respect and stature for the individual leading the effort. Instead of being seen by manufacturing as a bottleneck, the newly created Supplier Assurance function was seen as an aid in helping manufacturing achieve its production goals.

My earlier statistic of 80 percent of resistors changing toward being supportive means 20 percent will be resistant forever. This sadly was the case with the Receiving Inspection Vice President. You don't know when first dealing with Political Resistance if you are dealing with a hard-core resistor. You should always play the odds and assume they are one of the 80 percent.

What happens to the 20 percent of those hard-core resistors when you are successful with the 80 percent? First, these hard-core resistors attempt to recruit converts to their resistance. The old adage of "misery loves company" initially seems to apply. If you are not implementing the strategies mentioned in this chapter, these recruitment efforts will be successful. If most of the key stakeholders are moving toward the desired position on the Stakeholder Analysis Chart, then these hard-core resistors become "Covert Terrorists" and become ineffectual.

Think of the hard-core resistor discussing their resistance with someone starting to become committed to Six Sigma. Imagine the following discussion that could have transpired in our Receiving Inspection example:

> *Boy, these Six Sigma people are really screwing up things in our department. All this stuff is an excuse for these consultants to become rich.*

> *Oh, I don't know about that. That project we worked on with the Ajax supplier reduced defects so that we can go to direct shipments to the line. It's reducing our overtime and the project team enjoyed working with the supplier, teaching them Six Sigma methods rather than scolding them for bad product and sending their production lot back to them for re-sorting.*

While misery loves company, it is more accurate to say misery loves other miserable company. If your change efforts with those key stakeholders bear fruit, the hard-core resistors lose interest in recruitment. One of three things happens to these resistors.

Think of the organization successfully implementing Six Sigma as a fast-running stream. If momentum builds, then the resistor becomes like a rock in the river. One thing that happens is the river flows around the rock. This analogy indicates the resistor stays in the organization but becomes ineffectual.

In the worse-case scenario, one of two other things happen. If they don't find others in the organization who share similar opinions, resistors will attempt to find work in a non-Six Sigma company. In the worse-case scenario, the resistor is fired either for not supporting the Six Sigma effort or more likely for not carrying his normal workload.

I rarely suggest a termination. First, the odds are in your favor that the resistor will change. If properly administered, the odds are on your side. Thus, a termination may occur prior to the resistor becoming supportive. Second, if you are successfully working on other key stakeholders, the ineffectualness of the resistor becomes evident as key stakeholders move to their desired level of support.

However, if a resistor needs to be removed from the organization, make sure it's a public hanging. One adamant resistor noticeably removed due to his resistance efforts is usually the only involuntary termination you need to help expedite movement of other key stakeholders. But remember, do this as a last option, not a first option.

■ ORGANIZATIONAL RESISTANCE

The first two types of resistance result in primary strategies to do something *to* the resistor. In the last two types of resistance, part of our strategy is to do something to the Six Sigma initiative itself.

Organizational Resistance occurs when the change initiative removes the sense of control of the potential key stakeholder. There are some similarities between Political and Organizational Resistance. Once again, an overriding theme is loss or subtraction. While in Political Resistance the loss is positional, Organizational Resistance is associated more with pride, ego, and ownership of the change. An acronym closely associated with Organizational Resistance is NIH, which stands for Not Invented Here. The Organizational Resistor has a higher need for control over change than most. If the change is not their idea, they are preoccupied with the loss or subtraction they associate with the change.

One of my clients aggressively acquires other businesses. They usually target smaller companies, sometimes competitors. In one instance, the targeted company was a family-owned business that grew to such a level that they became a takeover target. Part of the enticement to the potential acquisition is the significant financial package offered to the targeted business as well as the ability to remain the business leader, albeit with approval decisions involving the parent organization.

My client has a company policy that all acquired businesses will embrace Six Sigma. I was called by my client to begin work with the newly acquired business. The business was formed in the 1950s by an entrepreneur who turned over the management reins to his oldest son (whom we will call Carl) in the 1980s. From interviews with key employees, past and present, I ascertained that Carl was highly competent. He had grown the business he inherited to such an extent that it was a takeover target of a Fortune 100 company. Adjectives that described the son included decisive, productive, hard-working, committed, intelligent, and forceful. Despite these strengths, he was also described as highly insecure. This was understandable. While highly skilled, Carl had inherited his father's business and was sensitive to the criticism that he was chosen because he was the son of the owner. The decision to be acquired had been influenced by the amazingly profitable terms of the merger and the ability to continue to manage the business with supervisory control by the acquiring organization.

We had difficulty from the start of Six Sigma implementation, in large part due to Carl. Six Sigma became the symbol of the acquisition. The acquisition, while having its positive elements, robbed Carl of the ability to exclusively call his own shots. The simple fact was that implementation of Six Sigma was a loss of his control over his own destiny, something that he was insecure about to begin with. Resistance to Six Sigma was overt, emotional, and expected.

Recognizing that the underlying issue of Organizational Resistance is control, pride, and sense of ownership, focus needs to be placed on modification of the change so that the key stakeholder feels greater control and a greater sense of ownership. Simply put, credit for the change needs to be the idea of the organizational resistor.

In this example, my strategy was two-fold. First, to modify the Six Sigma initiative in such a way as to have the initiative retain its integrity, yet have Carl be in control over its implementation. Second, to have him be involved in the early successes associated with Six Sigma.

This strategy worked to perfection. Knowing Carl needed ownership of Six Sigma, I inquired from him how the Six Sigma initiative, as practiced by the organization that acquired him, could have been better. His major issue was that too much time was spent on the creation of the infrastructure of Six Sigma. As noted in Chapter 2 of *The Six Sigma Revolution,* management must go through a series of steps that among other tasks help lead to strategic selection of projects. Carl thought this was at least initially unnecessary and he thought he knew areas of his business that Six Sigma projects could immediately improve.

I would have preferred for Carl to actively engage in the process management efforts prior to the creation of teams to practice Six Sigma tactics. At this point, it was important for *me* not to practice resistance. I was willing to modify the normal procedures so that Carl's resistance would begin to subside. However, like any good negotiation, I expected something in return for this modification. I asked him to personally be the sponsor (called the Champion as those who read *The Six Sigma Revolution* know) of two of the five initial tactical project improvement teams. This would accomplish two things. First, it would get Carl to personally involve himself in the Six Sigma initiative (which is one of the goals of the process management activities) and it would help me give Carl ownership of the successes of the Six Sigma projects.

Six months after we began the tactical elements of Six Sigma, Carl's projects were both successful, with cost savings that averaged $175,000 for each. This generated admiration and greater respect for Carl both within his own organization and among his new superiors. These successes resulted in Carl moving from someone being moderately against Six Sigma to being strongly supportive of Six Sigma. During the six months of being a Champion, I coaxed him into reading elements of my first book. At the conclusion of the first projects, he inquired into process management and we created the infrastructure albeit a few months later than normally recommended.

■ INDIVIDUALIZED RESISTANCE

In the late 1980s, a family-owned business in Wisconsin asked me to assist them implement the process management elements of Six Sigma. This manufacturing organization had grown in little more than 20 years to a multimillion dollar business. However, there are many organizations that learn the hard way that the skills needed to create a business are not necessarily the skills needed to sustain a business.

The company's founder and Chief Executive Officer asked me to begin working with them and shared financial information sufficient to conclude that they were on the verge of Chapter 11 Bankruptcy protection. Clearly, they had a short-term threat sufficient to create the need for a Six Sigma initiative. I began in earnest implementing the business process management elements that could salvage this company.

My work was exclusively with the executive team. With the executive team completely aware of the urgency of doing things differently, I had anticipated virtually no resistance. No resistance was visible in the early stages of implementing process management. By the fourth month in our consulting contract, it appeared that one of their vice presidents was being passively compliant with the six action items I had asked him to complete by that point of our consulting contract.

This vice president, whom we will call Patrick, was personally pleasant in all our conversations. There was no overt resistance to process management. Patrick said all the right things in all the right situations.

Finally, during a visit to upstate Wisconsin in month five of our contract, I asked him out to dinner. Over a bottle of wine, I inquired as to why his action items weren't further along. I felt I had asked this probing question somewhat diplomatically but his answer, fueled by alcohol, wasn't diplomatic at all.

"Why am I not further along in the implementation of your requests? I will tell you why. My wife just informed me she is divorcing me, my mother just died, I now have to put my father in a nursing home, and the only time I hear from my two children is when they call from college asking for money. Here you show up and are trying to change the only constant in my life."

Tempted to ask for either another bottle of wine or the check, I realized that this confession of how Patrick really felt was a sign of progress. Prior to this dinner, Patrick was a classic covert resistor, not expressing how he really felt but through behavior showing only a half-hearted effort. Now, through this confession, he was expressing his true feelings. It also represented a classic example of Individualized Resistance—resistance that comes when stress is at such a level that change results in emotional and sometimes behavioral paralysis.

I couldn't help but think back to the days when I taught psychology classes. During that time, I had come across a stress test. This test gave numerical values for certain life events associated with stress. Highest on the list was the death of a child. Second on the list was the divorce of a spouse and third on the list was the death of a parent. Adding all of Patrick's scores put him well past the threshold for life-threatening stress.

My psychology training had also taught me the typical reactions to such high stress. Like our story in Chapter 1 of the rat traversing the maze, psychological paralysis sets in, when faced with such life-altering change. Patrick's life was falling apart and the only constant he had was his job, which I was threatening to change.

When I pose this example to my class participants and ask what they would do, they invariably indicate that they would try to convince Patrick that unless he accommodates the changes asked of him relative to his job, he will experience even greater stress. This is technically a correct answer. However, this answer alone stands little chance of moving Patrick to the desired state of commitment. At some point, we would implement this strategy, but in the short term we need to implement two additional strategies when someone is experiencing Individualized Resistance.

First, we need to recognize the positive of Patrick becoming overt in sharing the high stress level he was currently experiencing. Only through empathizing with his current plight and developing some relationship with him will he ultimately hear the message of the need for him to change on the job.

Second, it is imperative that we modify the change expectations on Patrick. In this manner, Individual Resistance is similar to Organizational Resistance. Our short-term focus must be on modifying what is asked of the key stakeholder rather than doing something *to* the key stakeholder. In Patrick's case, I realized that I had asked him to complete six items within the first four months. This was under the assumption his stress level was within normal limits. In conjunction with the executive team (some of whom were or became aware of Patrick's life stresses), we temporarily removed some of the items on his plate relative to the change.

Within several months the short-term combination of less asked of him and the continuing rapport I was building with Patrick allowed us to take the next step to work on creating the need for him to take on more relative to the change. While still emotionally bruised, I stressed the WIIFM (What's in it for me), that class participants recommend to further move a key stakeholder to a desired position of support. By the end of my contract, Patrick was helping the change happen and we had recorded another success story of mobilizing commitment to Six Sigma change.

■ MULTIPLE RESISTANCE TO SIX SIGMA

The examples of resistance just discussed assume that each resistor is exhibiting one type of resistance. It is both possible and even likely that a person resistant to Six Sigma will experience and exhibit multiple types of resistance. If that is the case, it is recommended that the primary type of resistance be diagnosed. Then implement the strategy for that type of resistance first. If resistance is still evident after that, the secondary type of resistance strategy should be implemented, and so on.

■ SUMMARY

This chapter addressed the universal reaction to any change, which is seeing the change as loss. Loss breeds resistance to the change, particularly to Six Sigma, which, for most organizations, is a dramatic departure from how they have typically managed their businesses.

We discussed the importance of identifying the key stakeholders to the Six Sigma initiative. Once the key stakeholders have been identified, their current level of support needs to be established. There are five levels of support or nonsupport. After identifying where the key stakeholders are currently, we need to identify where they need to be if Six Sigma is to be successful. If there is a gap between the current and desired state of support to Six Sigma, it is likely there is some level of resistance that needs to be managed.

In this chapter, we identified four major types of resistance. We used four case studies of resistance. Table 3.3 shows how these four case studies would look.

The four major types of resistance are technical, political, organizational, and individual. Table 3.4 shows the underlying issues behind each type of resistance and the strategy to move your resistor to his or her desired state of support.

Despite these strategies, there will always be those individuals who resist Six Sigma. In Chapter 3 we discussed the three ways in which those who remain resistant to Six Sigma either leave the organization become ineffectual in their resistance, or as a last resort must be terminated.

Key Stakeholder	Strongly Against Having Six Sigma Happen	Moderately Against Having Six Sigma Happen	Lets Six Sigma Happen	Helps Six Sigma Happen	Makes Six Sigma Happen
George	O-----------	----------------------	----------------------	---------------	X
Vice President of Receiving Inspection	O-----------	----------------------	--------------	X	
Carl		O-----------	--------------	---------	X
Patrick		O-----------	--------------	---------	X

Table 3.3 Case studies—Stakeholder analysis chart.

Key Stakeholder	Type of Resistance	Underlying Issue(s)	Strategy to Combat the Resistance
George	Technical	Feelings of inadequacy, fear of feeling or looking stupid	Information Involvement Education
Vice President of Receiving Inspection	Political	Loss, real or perceived	Identification with the loss if real, stressing what is gained by the change rather than what is lost
Carl	Organizational	Issues of control, pride, and sense of ownership	Modification of the change effort, involvement of the resistor in the change so they can take ownership of the initiative
Patrick	Individual	Fear and emotional paralysis	Modification of the change to decrease the fear and increase involvement

Table 3.4 Issues behind types of resistance.

KEY LEARNINGS

➤ The universal reaction to change is loss.

➤ If the universal reaction to change is loss, resistance to the change should be expected.

➤ The first step in overcoming resistance is identification of the key stakeholders of the organization.

➤ After identification of the key stakeholders, we need to identify their current level of support or nonsupport to the Six Sigma initiative.

➤ There are five categories of support or nonsupport to Six Sigma. There are those that *make it happen* and those that *help it happen*. There are two major categories against Six Sigma, those *moderately against* and those *strongly against*. Finally, there are those that are *neutral* to Six Sigma.

➤ Once the current level of support or nonsupport for Six Sigma is charted, where each stakeholder needs to be if Six Sigma is to be successful needs to be established.

➤ For any gap between current and desired support, resistance may exist.

➤ There are four major types of resistance to Six Sigma:

1. *Technical resistance* occurs when Six Sigma produces feelings of inadequacy or perceptions of stupidity in the stakeholder.

2. *Political resistance* occurs when the stakeholder sees Six Sigma as a loss to him or her. This loss could be real or perceived.

3. *Organizational resistance* occurs when the stakeholder experiences issues of control, pride, and sense of loss of ownership over Six Sigma.

(continued)

(Continued)

    4. Finally, there are *individualized resistances* where stakeholders are experiencing fear and emotional paralysis, as a result of high stress.

➤ There are strategies to combat resistance. For technical resistance the strategy is information, education, and involvement. For political resistance to be overcome, identification with the loss is the first step in reducing or overcoming political resistance. In addition, stressing the addition that Six Sigma brings to the stakeholder must be established. For organizational resistance, modification of the Six Sigma initiative is recommended so that the cultural resistor has greater control over the initiative. Finally, for individual resistance, modification of the change to decrease the fear and increase involvement is recommended.

Chapter 4

Molding the
Six Sigma Vision,
Results, and Behaviors

This book is not written linearly. Change agents are not expected to complete the items in Chapter 3 before dealing with Chapter 4 and so on. For that matter, the change agent may decide that once the need for Six Sigma is created, they would immediately move to implementing *molding the vision,* the topic of this chapter.

This chapter on molding the Six Sigma Vision focuses on three elements. First, we will discuss what is the vision of a Six Sigma culture. Once we create a need for change and have our key stakeholders ready to charge up the proverbial hill, we better have the right hill for our people to charge up. In the beginning of this chapter, we will talk about what the vision of a Six Sigma culture is all about.

Having a Six Sigma Vision is not enough. Once we understand what the vision of a Six Sigma culture is, we need to create the goals and mindset of those we expect to change toward a Six Sigma culture.

Finally, and most important, once we create the need for change it is vital to describe the type of changing behaviors you can expect in a Six Sigma culture. To improve the acceptance of Six Sigma (the A in $Q \times A$ in Chapter 1), a critical piece is the formulation of the vision, goals, and behaviors that await those who move toward changing the way a Six Sigma organization operates.

In this chapter we establish ways to create the vision, results, and behaviors of a Six Sigma organization. We conclude the chapter with how to "pitch" Six Sigma to other employees in the organization. Finally, we review typical questions that those who are resistant to Six Sigma have and comment on answers most executives provide.

■ THE VISION OF THE SIX SIGMA CULTURE

In my seminars with executives, I begin this section of the course by drawing the bull's-eye that you see in Figure 4.1. The bull's-eye has four rings and a black target. The outer ring represents the vision of the Six Sigma culture.

I tell class participants to begin with the outer ring. I ask them to write words they associate with the vision of the Six Sigma culture. The more frequent responses I have received over the years include:

➤ Improvement

➤ Data

➤ Facts

➤ Process

➤ Customer

➤ Employees

➤ Analysis

➤ Measurement

Figure 4.1 Bulls-Eye

➤ Projects

➤ Perfection

➤ Never-ending

➤ Defects

Once they have exhausted listing the words that come to mind, I ask each executive to create phrases or sentences using as many of the words as possible. Typical phrases or sentences include:

➤ Customer-focused improvement.

➤ Process improvement through fact-based analysis.

➤ Process improvement projects aimed at defect reduction.

➤ Customer, process, and employee focus.

➤ Striving for never-ending improvement toward reducing defects.

➤ Fact-based measurement.

➤ Seeking perfection in all processes.

➤ Meet and exceed customer needs and requirements.

➤ Effectiveness and efficiency.

The next step is to create the Six Sigma mission for the organization. I subdivide the executive team into small groups of 3 to 5. I then ask them to take the aforementioned phrases and attempt to create a mission statement combining the more relevant phrases according to each subgroup. I stress to each subgroup of executives not to spend valuable time word-smithing the mission statement. This can be done later once agreement on the phrases is reached. Next are listed some of the better mission statements that executive subgroups have created:

➤ Six Sigma is the prevailing management philosophy of _____. Our mission through Six Sigma is to create a customer-focused culture dedicated to never-ending improvement in all we do. This will be accomplished through fact-based measurement and attempting to achieve perfection in all processes.

➤ Our mission is to be a customer, process, and employee-focused organization. Six Sigma will help us accomplish this through practicing fact-based measurement in our goal of reducing defects in all our processes.

➤ The mission of _____ is to improve productivity and profitability through Six Sigma. Six Sigma will be our management philosophy, ensuring process improvement that will result in greater effectiveness and efficiency.

➤ We at _____ are committed to utilizing Six Sigma to achieve improved productivity, greater customer satisfaction, superior process management, and challenged, though satisfied, employees.

■ THE GOALS OF SIX SIGMA

Creating the Six Sigma Vision involves work. The exercise just discussed helps the executive team see what they want their organization to be like once a need for Six Sigma is created. The next level in the bull's-eye analogy attempts to identify the goals for the Six Sigma culture.

Here we begin to quantify what implementing the Six Sigma Vision will accomplish. Once again, I have the executives answer the following question, "What goals or mindset will be in place once the Six Sigma Vision is implemented?" As in a previous exercise, I hand out some sticky notes and have them capture one idea per note. The most common responses are:

➤ 3.4 defects per million opportunities.

➤ 24-hour customer response time.

➤ First call customer resolution.

➤ Best-in-class customer satisfaction.

➤ Less than 10 percent inefficiency in any process.

➤ Less than 10 percent annualized employee turnover.

➤ No recall of product.

➤ No customer complaints.

➤ First time introduction of production.

➤ Six Sigma.

One client example of both a Vision and Goals is:

The _____ Six Sigma Vision: The mission of _____ is to improve productivity and profitability through Six Sigma. Six Sigma will be our management philosophy, ensuring process improvement that will result in greater effectiveness and efficiency.

The _____ Six Sigma Goals to be achieved by Year 2003:

1. *We will move from third place (out of five competitors) to first in customer satisfaction.*

2. *We will reduce our inefficiency rating from its current level of 43 percent to less than 10 percent.*

3. *Our annualized employee turnover will be reduced to single digits.*

■ THE BEHAVIORS OF A SIX SIGMA CULTURE

In 1999, the bombing on Kosovo took place. It was unusual warfare in that it was done without ground troops. Various bombers took off from aircraft carriers in the Mediterranean and bombed various targets in and around Kosovo. One thing was certain among the pilots: they all reported they received flak when they were over the target. This same analogy is true when you gain agreement on the behaviors that will change in a Six Sigma culture.

The exercise of gaining agreement on the mission, the goals, and behaviors of a Six Sigma organization is an exercise I practice each year with my family. Those of you who read *The Six Sigma Revolution* remember the Eckes family used the tools and techniques each year to select a summer vacation. Each January we craft our family mission and establish goals for each family member as well as general family goals. Last year Joe indicated he would like to see "more family time" established as a family goal.

"More family time" was quickly registered as a goal and we returned to it when we were attempting to operationally define the behavior(s) of what "more family time" would look like as a behavior. Like our two previous exercises, I ask each person to write down what a behavior for a given goal would look like. My son Temo wrote the following:

Goal	Behavior
More family time.	Dad will put down the TV clicker and come out and play with us.

From the above you can clearly see that the behavior is "over the target." It was easy for me to agree to "more family time," just as it will be for your organization to agree to a goal of improved customer responsiveness. You will know that you have identified behaviors when there is either "push-back" to the idea, overt criticism, or in my situation a recognition of a behavior that needed to be changed.

Several years ago I was doing this exercise with a noted computer manufacturer. The exercise had gone well through the first two phases. Highest among the list of goals was to be "more customer focused in all we do." There was no disagreement with this goal. After agreement on their list of goals, I then instructed this executive group to write behaviors for each prioritized list of goals. I vividly remember the reaction of the group as I read off the first card for everyone's clarification:

No more empty boxes.

An audible moan went through this group. At this point I had no idea what an empty box was and so I asked for clarification. The response was a stunner:

We have struggled for years to meet Wall Street's expectations of us relative to stock price. To meet our revenue promises, we have historically shipped the computer "shell" (the box), fully aware that the internal workings of the computer would not be functional. We were able to register the box as shipped revenue, then send out our field engineers to wire the box to make it functional after it had been marked as shipped revenue.

The "discussion" that ensued was both lively and heated. The results were not decided that day. However, over a series of meetings that this company asked me to facilitate, a key behavior that changed was "No more empty boxes."

■ MORE OF / LESS OF

A tool I suggest teams utilize throughout the three phases of creation of the Six Sigma Vision is to have participants think in terms of what they will have *more of* and what the organization will have *less of.*

Relative to either goals or behaviors, thinking in terms of more of/less of can assist executive teams through the three exercises mentioned in this chapter.

■ THE "ELEVATOR SPEECH"

At General Electric, there is the concept of the "Elevator Speech." In relation to Six Sigma, the Elevator Speech refers to what a leader would say should he or she get on an elevator with a peer or subordinate who asks about Six Sigma. Specifically, in the 90 seconds or so you might be in the elevator with this peer or subordinate, an executive would expect to comment briefly on:

➤ What Six Sigma is.

➤ Why General Electric was embracing Six Sigma as a management philosophy.

➤ The benefits of Six Sigma.

➤ What is expected of the peer or subordinate relative to Six Sigma.

In my Six Sigma change seminar, I have executives find a partner. I then have them take a half hour or so and write a Six Sigma Elevator Speech. Then in the next half hour, I have them make their "pitch" to their partner. The partner is told to be either neutral, or in voluntary cases requested by an executive, be moderately resistant. During the pitch, the partner reflects on the message and at the end of the pitch provides feedback to the partner. First, the recipient of the pitch tells the pluses of the message, then provides "deltas", which are suggestions for improvement.

Once everyone has gone through both pitching and hearing a pitch, I ask for a volunteer to give a Six Sigma Elevator Speech that went well so that all can hear. Here are two of the better ones I have heard:

Six Sigma is the management philosophy we have adopted to become a more effective, efficient organization. It is an approach for us to identify the customers throughout our business, find out their needs and requirements, measure our current performance, and empower our employees to find ways to improve performance. Successful Six Sigma performance will result in greater customer satisfaction, which will result in keeping current customers and finding new ones. It empowers employees to improve the processes they work in which will result in greater employee satisfaction. Your role in leading Six Sigma is crucial. You will be expected to learn how to measure key variables that drive performance in the processes you work in and find out about ways to improve the process. When you do, you will find greater work performance, greater work life balance, and less stress in your job.

In the second example, the Elevator Speech was more of a dialogue. The participants got off on the same floor and continued their discussion:

Joan, you just got out of that Six Sigma training I have been hearing about. Was it as bad as you thought?

Ted, I learned a lot about becoming more effective and efficient. I really think this approach to our business could be the vehicle to take us to the next level of growth. Ted, what frustrates you most in your job?

This last question is a stroke of genius. For starters, it's a great way to start a dialogue. I have yet to run into any person who, when asked this question, doesn't have to be cut off eventually. People are faced with many different frustrations in their jobs which results in plenty of discussion. Second, by allowing them to talk about their frustrations, they will eventually lead the elevator speaker to streamline and personalize the message to the stakeholder to whom the Elevator Speech is aimed. Ted went on to respond,

> *I spend at least two hours a day redoing those TPS reports that Joe (in Finance) requires. Then I circulate them to Dom in Logistics and Debbie in Master Scheduling. I don't think they even pay attention to the changes, it's a waste of my time. Then I waste another two hours every other week writing my bimonthly activity report, which is an exercise in creative writing. Hey, what does all this have to do with Six Sigma anyway?*

Joan responds,

> *It seems all of us have those inefficiencies that seem to occupy our days. What I have learned is that Six Sigma is a method to streamline the processes in our business so that we spend more time efficiently serving the needs of the customer, even those internal customers to our business. Six Sigma is a way to make our lives easier, helping to identify the important things we need to be working on and learning to do them better and more effectively.*

➤ Elevator Speech Questions

One benefit that has come out of my Elevator Speech exercise is seeing how the participants become emotional with regard to trying to "win over" the partner to whom they are giving the Six Sigma Elevator Speech. Even in cases where I have suspected that the executive is neutral to moderately against Six Sigma, the natural competitive juices seem to flow and they actually request the person to whom they give the speech to exhibit some moderate resistance to Six Sigma.

As a result, I have been witness to some great dialogues (sometimes looking more like debates) around issues that perhaps originally both participants shared as forms of resistance. I have collected some of the better questions that are raised against Six Sigma which can be seen as forms of resistance and the excellent answers that were provided in the Elevator Speech exercise. I have tried to list them in terms of the questions I typically have heard, from the most common to some of the more unique ones. I will then take each question, provide one way to answer the question, and comment on the question.

1. Takes too long.

2. Isn't it cost ineffective to obtain Six Sigma?

3. Lots of statistics.

4. We are unique.

5. Projects take forever.

6. I don't have time to work on the projects.

7. No formal processes.

8. This works better in manufacturing.

9. This is just another fad.

10. We have tried this before.

11. Management won't support it.

12. Too many tools.

13. This doesn't work in education or government.

14. Six Sigma will sap my organization of its creativity.

1. Six Sigma Cultural Transformation Takes Too Long.

Answer: To achieve a Six Sigma cultural transformation for most organizations will take two to five years normally. Early successes showing the benefits of Six Sigma can and do occur within six months of starting an initiative. The length of time to achieve a cultural transformation is based on the degree of current inefficiency and ineffectiveness in the organization and the degree of commitment of management and worker alike. Remember, things that are worthwhile don't happen overnight. Whether it's getting in shape, raising a child, or finding a dream job, if something is important, it may take some time, particularly if you have been doing the wrong things for a period of time.

Comment: When this question is posed to me in a class, I attempt to read body language or connect this question to previous questions asked by the participant. In some cases, it is a legitimate question. In other cases, I describe the question as an "Iceberg" question where the participant is venting her or his frustration. In the former case, I spend more time on the beginning of the answer; in the latter case, I try to get the participant talking about anything she or he has done worthwhile and how long it took. Besides, if a Six Sigma consultant promised a panacea to transform a business in weeks, wouldn't he or she be considered a bit of a snake oil salesperson?

2. Isn't It Going to Cost More to Achieve Six Sigma Quality Than I Am Going to Get in Return?

Answer: First, do you know how much it is costing you to not be a Six Sigma organization? Have you lost a customer recently due to poor product or service performance? Do you have any idea of the cost of inefficient processes related to elements such as rework, scrap, machine downtime, excessive inventory, customer complaints, warranty costs, and the like?

Second, since most companies today are in the two to three sigma performance range as an overall organization, this tends to be more of a hypothetical question until you are at four to five sigma as an organization. And since this will take you years to accomplish, in some ways this is a premature question.

Finally, if you think it will "cost" you to achieve Six Sigma, make sure you have no competitors who are pursuing Six Sigma. There are several examples of companies who were considered first in their field until a competitor implemented Six Sigma and leap-frogged over them in terms of customer loyalty.

Comment: Typically, this question is an Iceberg question coming from a moderately to strongly resistant stakeholder. When the question comes from a more neutral participant, the strongly worded answer has proved helpful in getting the questioner to respond later to me that he didn't think of the costs of not being a Six Sigma organization. If this question comes from someone who is strongly resistant, answering this question in this manner can have greater impact on those around the resistor than the resistor himself.

3. There Seems to Be Too Much Emphasis on Statistics

Answer: The math associated with Six Sigma is basically addition and subtraction. Your biggest challenge will be changing to making decisions with facts and data. This will take time but eventually will benefit everyone in the organization. When you make decisions without data, you are at the mercy of chance. The Six Sigma organization makes its decisions on data.

Comment: Some clients have had previous experience with Six Sigma consultants who think Six Sigma is all about statistics and theorems. If this is the case, I give a little more slack in my answer. If this is not the case, the underlying issue usually is transforming the organization from one that uses "gut feel" and experience as their primary decision-making method to data-based decision making. Thus, the appropriate answer is to recognize the math in Six Sigma as being relatively simple and focus on the Six Sigma organization being based on fact-based decision making.

4. We Are Unique and Six Sigma Would Not Work in This Environment

Answer: Every organization that has implemented Six Sigma is unique in its own way. Every organization will have unique challenges in implementing Six Sigma. These challenges must be identified and overcome. However, if you have a product or service, then you have customers who have requirements that must be met. At its basic level, Six Sigma is attempting to use facts and data to drive customer satisfaction. If you don't have a product or service or you don't have customers, then you might be right.

Comments: Depending on the client, I sometimes answer facetiously that if I had a nickel for every time I have heard this question I would drive a midnight blue Porsche 911 Carrera. In reality, I tone down the true answer for this question. In 20 years of consulting, I have met few truly unique business cultures. Regardless of any culture's unique quality, this answer is quite on the mark. If you have customers you provide a product or service to, you can (and should) implement Six Sigma. Underlying this question is the lame attempt to avoid change by claiming anything that worked for somebody else couldn't possibly work for them.

5. *Projects Take Forever*

Answer: First projects will take approximately six months from inception to implementation of the Control phase. Recognize that one big factor that contributes to this time line is that in addition to improving a process that in all likelihood is a poor performing process, the team is also learning a new methodology for improvement.

Comments: I sometimes augment this answer with a quick exercise. I ask everyone to take out a piece of paper, take a pen or pencil in their nondominant hand and write out their signature as if they are signing a check. Laughter rings out as they finish this assignment and inspect their work. I then tell them to sign their "John Hancock" as they would normally. Then, I ask them to comment on their two writing experiences. Invariably, the de-brief of this quick exercise is that the first experience was not as polished as their normal way of doing things, that it felt more awkward, and that the first time took much longer to complete. The second time it was easier and better.

I concentrate on the last point. Whenever you do something new it will usually take longer. At this point, I tell the story of my dear departed mother who, like her son, was born left-handed. In the early part of the twentieth century, being left-handed was considered evil (the Italian word for left is *sinistre* or "sinister"). The nuns teaching her forced my mom to write with her right hand. She became so ambidextrous she was able to write with both hands simultaneously. What I stress to my class participants is that her ability to do this didn't happen right away.

6. I Don't Have Time to Work on the Projects

Answer: Why is it we never seem to have time to improve a process but we always seem to have time to do something over and over again until it is done right? Do you have any idea of the amount of time you spend inefficiently that impacts your work performance and even your personal time? If we don't spend time improving processes, they become more and more inefficient resulting in less effectiveness provided to the customer and more time to perform the activities in the process.

Do you run your car every day until it breaks down without spending some time on preventive maintenance? Or do you budget some time to have your car oil changed and engine tuned? Think of how a car would run if you never had it maintained? Or what if your job was chopping down trees, but you never spent time sharpening your ax? You would think of people who did this as relatively stupid. Yet, somehow the concept of maintenance or ax sharpening doesn't apply to our jobs. Perhaps it *should* apply to our jobs.

Comments: This is a commonly asked question, yet I haven't overcome my frustration with it. Of course, it is usually a reflection of the current management culture which doesn't see process improvement as part of the job description. We address this need in Chapter 6, *Measuring the Six Sigma Culture.*

7. We Don't Have Any Processes

Answer: Unless this organization is equivalent to Michelangelo creating the *Sistine Chapel* one day and the *Pieta* the next, you have processes. Remember our definition of a process: a series of steps and activities that take inputs provided by suppliers, and produce an output or outputs for a customer. In all likelihood, you have not formalized or named your processes, but virtually everything a business does involves a process.

Comments: The focus of this answer has to be on recognizing that the participant is unaware of their processes or doesn't recognize that many of their processes are currently informal processes. It should also be noted that in many cases the answer will be created by asking questions of the participant to get them to discover their processes by asking more of what they do every day.

8. This Only Works in Manufacturing

Answer: There are advantages and disadvantages to implementation of Six Sigma in manufacturing. Among the disadvantages is getting the manufacturing process to "talk" to you. It's equivalent to being a veterinarian and diagnosing an animal's illness. In the service industry, you get to talk to people in the process to find out what is happening, but in manufacturing you have to conduct tests like Designed Experiments to get the process to talk to you through data. Everyone has challenges in implementing Six Sigma, but it is not a question of working in one type of industry versus another.

Comments: Of course when I visit a manufacturing organization, I often hear just the opposite question (i.e., this only works in service-related businesses). It is important in answering this type of question to acknowledge that each organization will have certain advantages and disadvantages in implementing Six Sigma. Once this is acknowledged, it is then important to cite one disadvantage that another client had that the current client doesn't have.

9. *This Is Just Another Quality Fad*

Answer: While there are similarities between Six Sigma and other quality initiatives, there are critical differences as well. First and foremost are the results. While previous quality efforts were well intentioned, they often fell short of contributing to the bottom line. AlliedSignal has saved over $1 billion since they began Six Sigma in the early 1990s. General Electric has improved both their effectiveness and efficiency to the tune of over $1 billion in less time than AlliedSignal. In the case of General Electric, they have implemented other quality initiatives with limited success, but nothing like the results they have generated with Six Sigma.

Second, in direct relationship to the results that Six Sigma has generated, upper management has shown interest in Six Sigma unlike their interest in any other quality initiative. Third, Six Sigma addresses both tactical improvement similar to other quality initiatives, yet also is comprised of a strategic component, Business Process Management (Chapter 2 in *The Six Sigma Revolution*). Fourth, Six Sigma methodology has the rigor and discipline that most other quality initiatives lack.

Comments: Six Sigma does utilize many of the tools and techniques of other quality initiatives. In my years of consulting, I have consulted in Total Quality Management, Statistical

Process Control, and others, yet Six Sigma has produced more benefits to my clients in a shorter period of time while garnering higher involvement of management, which is crucial for any change initiative to work.

10. We Have Tried This Before

Answer: The important issue is to build Six Sigma into your current or previous efforts at improving productivity in your organization. Tell me about your current/previous effort and how it has been successful and how it could have been better?

Comments: The critical issue behind answering this question is found in the second sentence. In most cases, there have been previous efforts. Sadly, most of these previous efforts have been unsuccessful. It is important to recognize previous efforts. First, from a psychological perspective, previous efforts must be lauded, particularly if the questioner was a part of that effort. Second, it is critical at some point, if the effort was unsuccessful, to do a brief failure analysis and contrast how Six Sigma will be different. In these situations, I end up leading the group to the understanding that previous efforts probably were deficient in the A of the $Q \times A$ formula.

11. Management Won't Support It

Answer: Management won't support something that doesn't contribute to the bottom line. This is another area where Six Sigma is different than other quality initiatives. Even at the tactical level, projects must be selected that have high impact on the strategic business objectives of the organization. Improvement efforts that result in positive movement of such strategic business objectives as revenue will gain the attention of business leaders furthering the support of the Six Sigma effort.

Comments: Management will not nor should not support quality efforts that don't contribute to the bottom line. When we treat management as a key stakeholder and identify their issues with a quality initiative, we will be much further along than if we assume management should blindly support the Six Sigma effort.

12. Too Many Tools

Answer: There is an old adage that says when your only tool is a hammer, every problem looks like a nail. It is critically important to note that through the application of the process improvement methodology (DMAIC), or the process design methodology (DMADV), there are a host of tools available to the project team. However, once a tool has been learned well enough to apply it to the project, it doesn't necessarily mean it should be used. Think of the tools associated with Six Sigma as belonging in a tool box. Just because you have both a regular screwdriver and a Phillips screwdriver doesn't mean you use both. For example, mastery of a box plot and a histogram should result in use of one, not both.

Comments: Questions of this type reflect technical resistance. Remember that over the long haul, information, involvement, and education about the tools are the best way to reduce or eliminate this type of resistance.

13. This Doesn't Work in Education or Government

Answer: If you can make the case that in both education and government there are no customers with needs and requirements, then I would have to agree.

Comments: Eckes and Associates, Inc. worked in the early 1990s with government clients as part of Al Gore's Reinventing Government initiative. While there were exceptions, it was one of the most frustrating consulting experiences I have had. Resistance to improvement was rampant and little need was created for change. While some improvements ensued, it didn't work well in government because government management and workers had a tough time identifying who the customer was. The same could be said for some initiatives in education. Who is the customer in education? Is it the student? If so, what would we say if some twelfth graders said their requirements were less homework? While improvements in the effectiveness and efficiency of our education process is vital, a Six Sigma approach can prove challenging.

14. Six Sigma Will Sap My Organization of Its Creativity

Answer: Just the opposite is true. Six Sigma will provide those whose creativity has been hampered by inefficiency and bureaucracy to flourish through either process improvement or process design. Particularly with a process design project, the creativity of project team members can be harnessed through the methodology. Creativity isn't stifled with Six Sigma, it thrives.

Comment: True creativity is benefited by Six Sigma as the answer illustrates. In answering this question, it is important to ascertain whether it is creativity that the questioner is concerned with or relinquishing decision-making authority. If it is the latter, remember our answer to Question 3. The underlying issue usually is transforming the organization from one that uses "gut feel" and experience as their primary decision-making method. Thus, the appropriate answer is to recognize that the math in Six Sigma is relatively simple and focus on the Six Sigma organization being based on fact-based decision making.

■ SUMMARY

Once the need for change toward Six Sigma is created, it is vital to create the Six Sigma Vision. This Vision stresses what the mission of a Six Sigma organization looks like; second, it is important to identify the goals of a Six Sigma organization; and finally, what the behaviors look like in a successful Six Sigma culture.

Suggestions for how a Six Sigma Vision can be created were suggested. How to incorporate the Vision into an Elevator Speech was discussed. Finally, the most typical questions that I have faced as a Six Sigma consultant were given with answers and comments. These answers work best with those who are neutral or moderately resistant to Six Sigma and only rarely with those who are strongly resistant.

KEY LEARNINGS

➤ Once the need for Six Sigma is created, the organization needs to know what a Six Sigma organization looks like in terms of vision, results, and behaviors.

➤ This chapter addressed highly pragmatic ways to create a viable Six Sigma mission statement.

➤ Once a mission has been created, the results of a Six Sigma organization must be envisioned.

➤ The last and most important element of creating the Six Sigma Vision is to create those behaviors that exhibit itself in a Six Sigma culture.

(continued)

(Continued)

➤ Once the vision, results, and behaviors of a Six Sigma culture are created, key executives in the organization must create a consistent Elevator Speech that answers the questions: What is Six Sigma? Why is the organization embracing Six Sigma as a management philosophy? What are the benefits of Six Sigma? What behaviors are expected of the peer or subordinate relative to Six Sigma?

➤ In the course of dealing with the Six Sigma Vision, employees of the organization will have many questions about Six Sigma. Some of these questions will be forms of resistance. Other times these questions will be honest skepticism. Regardless, it provides the first opportunity to address employees' questions that can allow for Six Sigma to become a cultural phenomenon.

Chapter 5

Creating the
Six Sigma Culture

Approximately 30 percent of my clients have obtained a true cultural transformation with Six Sigma. For a client to be mentioned as a true Six Sigma success story, the elements discussed in this chapter need to embraced.

The elements of this chapter address culture strategically. They uniformly center on the various systems and structures that either will support or hinder the Six Sigma behaviors we referenced in Chapter 4. Think of this chapter as assisting you in the creation of the infrastructure that will make Six Sigma more than just a cost-savings initiative in your business.

Specifically, there are six major elements that either need to be created or modified for Six Sigma to thrive in your organization. Virtually all of them are the domain of management. As such, this chapter may be the most important one for executives to read and adhere to once they are committed to implementing Six Sigma in their organization.

The six systems and structures covered in this chapter are:

1. How to hire Six Sigma people in your organization.

2. How to develop Six Sigma people in your organization.

3. How to evaluate Six Sigma behaviors in your organization.

4. How to reward and recognize Six Sigma behaviors.

5. How to communicate Six Sigma in your organization.

6. How to change job structures in your organization strategically (Business Process Management) and tactically (Six Sigma Job Descriptions, Roles, and Responsibilities).

This chapter describes the key Six Sigma positions in an organization and the type of people who should fill them. This includes who should be the Quality Leader for your organization and what core competencies they should possess. We talk about how to interview and hire your external consultant.

We address how to educate the organization about Six Sigma. Specifically, we inform you of the types of training courses you should offer your employees. We share with you our training secrets that enabled us to become GE Capital's highest rated consultants.

In addition, we discuss how to evaluate employees in your organization relative to Six Sigma, whether they be top executives or individual contributors. Reward and recognition is important to any change initiative. We discuss in this chapter what works and what doesn't work.

Communication is critical to the success of any Six Sigma initiative. We discuss various venues for Six Sigma communication to assist in helping sustain Six Sigma. Finally, we discuss how job structures should be modified to sustain Six Sigma.

■ HIRING SIX SIGMA PEOPLE IN YOUR ORGANIZATION

The client I experienced the least resistance with was the Westin Tabor Center in Denver. I once asked Bill Dougherty, their general manager, why this was the case. He had a simple but powerful answer. He hires open-minded, customer-oriented people with a propensity to learn new ideas. Little of the issues of resistance we discussed in Chapter 3 were present with the Westin Tabor Center.

In part I think the low resistance experienced at the Westin was due to Bill Dougherty's interview skills. Think of how interviews were conducted 10 to 15 years ago. A nearly uniform set of questions were asked about computer skills. These questions were asked because the organization wanted to insure that those coming on board had these skills rather than hiring someone only to have to train them on computer skills. Not only were questions asked about computer skills but it was a factor in the hiring decision. The organization of 10 to 15 years ago was communicating to potential hires that this was an expectation of every potential hire. Thus, one major structure I strongly recommend to organizations to adopt is to include a set of mandatory questions regarding previous quality experience or aptitude toward quality improvement. Furthermore, quality criteria, just like computer skills, should be a consideration in the hiring process. This needs to be done at the strategic level in coordination with Human Resources.

This is even more important when interviewing for the key Six Sigma positions. There are several major Six Sigma positions. We discuss them next.

➤ The Quality Leader

The Quality Leader is usually a vice president, a key position within the executive board. The Quality Leader should preferably be someone who has been in an executive position within the organization for some time and has both generated results and has the respect of peers and subordinates. Gone are the days where the quality function is given to a former business leader who has been sent "out to pasture" where both the business and the individual was content to guide a poorly respected but necessary function. Today, the Quality Leader position is a pivotally important post.

The Quality Leader must have the skills necessary to create and sustain Six Sigma without being afraid to take chances, or "rock the boat." When an organization initiates a Six Sigma effort, employees will be closely monitoring management's commitment and involvement. Leadership is crucial and the Quality Leader's job will be to ensure that all executives are directly involved in the quality effort. I vividly remember W. Edwards Deming (the noted quality consultant who died in 1993) telling me that at the beginning of a quality initiative management is "unconsciously incompetent," or as General Electric puts it, "they don't know what they don't know." In the early stages of the Six Sigma effort, it is the job of the Quality Leader to create a sense of urgency about management's involvement in Six Sigma. If the Quality Leader is too politically sensitive, he or she may allow the executive team to see Six Sigma as nothing more than a cost-saving initiative derived by putting teams through a series of cost-saving tactical projects. This approach is a serious mistake. Six Sigma is first and foremost a management philosophy. If management thinks any other way, the best that can be expected is tactical results which at best last a year or so because teams don't see the other benefits derived from a Six Sigma culture. Project teams will fail in their subsequent efforts as participants begin to see Six Sigma as nothing more than another vehicle to "get more work out of the employees."

Good Quality Leaders have a variety of core competencies. While embracing change, they are cognizant of the current culture. While recognizing the need for change, they also understand the personalities of the various other executives on the team. They know when to push but they should also know when to back off. This is yet another reason that the Quality Leader should be chosen from the current executive team. To bring in an outsider, even an outsider with considerable quality experience, is often a mistake because having the rapport and respect of someone within the current executive team is far more important than the knowledge of the details of Six Sigma. In addition, the Quality Leader must be able to think and manage strategically. The first and foremost responsibility of the Quality Leader is to assist the executive team in creating the Business Process Management System.* Virtually all of the elements in Business Process Management are strategic in nature and as such the Quality Leader must have the vision, respect, and strategic thinking to complete this most important step in the Six Sigma journey.

I have been fortunate to have worked closely with several Six Sigma vice presidents who both meet, and, in some cases, exceed these requirements. Janet Burki at GE Access, Judith Milsaps of GE TIP in Philadelphia, Debbie Neuscheler of GE

---

*For a thorough understanding of Business Process Management read Chapters 2 and 9 of *The Six Sigma Revolution: How General Electric and Others Turned Process Into Profits.*

Modular Space in Philadelphia, and Michelle Landis of GE CEF. To these fine leaders, I would also add Bill Brubaker of Volvo Trucks North America and Guenter Bulk of GE Compunet in Frankfurt, Germany. One of the most competent Quality Leaders I have worked with is Jack Becker of Lithonia Lighting headquartered in Atlanta, Georgia. His leadership skills are so pronounced I highlight his story in a later chapter in this book.

➤ The Master Black Belt

The terminology of karate was first used to describe levels of expertise at Motorola during Six Sigma's inception in the 1980s. The Master Black Belt is the highest level of mastery of the tools, techniques, and concepts associated with Six Sigma. The Master Black Belt operates as the internal quality consultant, coaching teams, providing tutorials, and facilitating meetings with both project teams and executives alike.

The skill set necessary to be an accomplished Master Black Belt is both technical and strategic in nature. The foundation of any good Master Black Belt is his or her technical skills. Table 5.1 lists the specific skill areas in which any Master Black Belt should be competent.

Sadly, most businesses simply look at a Master Black Belt potential hire from the perspective of their ability to manage the technical aspects of teams. This is both inaccurate and potentially fatal to the organization.

The better Master Black Belts I have worked with have a myriad of responsibilities. They assist teams with their work, often being an ad hoc member of teams working through either a process improvement or process design project.

However, the real worth of a Master Black Belt is utilizing their skill set at the strategic level as well. A skilled Black Belt can assist the executive leadership team with their new

Strategic and Tactical Skills	Cultural Skills	Facilitative Skills
➤ Knowledge of core, key sub, and enabling processes. ➤ Knowledge of how to brainstorm and assist management with project selection criteria. ➤ Knowledge of how to charter a team. ➤ Knowledge of how to acquire and validate customer needs and requirements. ➤ Knowledge of how to map a process at both a high and detailed level. ➤ Knowledge of how to create and implement a data collection plan. ➤ Knowledge on how to calculate Six Sigma, both the discrete and continuous way. ➤ Knowledge on how to conduct data analysis, process analysis, and root cause analysis. ➤ Mastery of how to set up/execute/analyze an experiment. ➤ Knowledge of how to generate, select and implement solutions to improve sigma performance. ➤ Knowledge of what type of control method is best for each project and how to create and sustain a Response Plan.	➤ Knowledge of how to create the need for Six Sigma strategically and how to create the need for solutions on project teams. ➤ Knowledge of how to shape a vision of Six Sigma for a project team and for the entire Six Sigma effort at the executive level. ➤ Knowledge of how to create buy-in for Six Sigma, specifically the ability to diagnose the four major types of resistance, their underlying issues and strategies to overcome resistance. ➤ Knowledge of how to overcome resistance to project solutions. ➤ How to advise executive teams on how to change their systems and structures to ensure adoption of Six Sigma and completion of Six Sigma projects. ➤ Knowledge of how to coach executive leaders on how to create, manage, and lead a Six Sigma initiative.	➤ Knowledge on how to set agendas, determine outcomes for meetings, assist a group in setting ground-rules and operating agreements. ➤ Knowledge of how to agree on roles and responsibilities for a meeting, specifically the facilitator, scribe, timekeeper. ➤ Knowledge of the difference between low and higher level interventions and when to employ both.

Table 5.1 Master Black Belt skill areas.

responsibilities. This includes aiding the executives with process management activities. This also includes core process identification, key subprocess dashboard creation and validation. In addition, Master Black Belt assistance includes helping executives learn new methods of facilitative leadership that should apply as much to how an executive runs a staff meeting as to how it should be applied to a Six Sigma project improvement team.

This means that Master Black Belts must have several key skill sets. First and foremost, they must have mastered any and all technical skills associated with both the strategic and tactical elements of Six Sigma. This is the foundation of their skill sets. Knowing when to apply a Designed Experiment and how to calculate Six Sigma is only the beginning. A talented Master Black Belt must have superb communication skills. It is one thing to know the difference between a core process and an enabling process or the difference between discrete versus continuous data. However, the ability to communicate that knowledge is a far more critical ability.

One of the best Master Black Belts I have encountered is Cedric Brown of Lithonia Lighting. Within the last several years Cedric has honed his inherent intelligence to master virtually every technical tool and technique. Thus, the first of the skill sets of technical mastery was established early on for Cedric. Yet, for people like Cedric, mastery of the technical tools was just the beginning of the mastery of his craft.

My involvement with Lithonia Lighting began in 1999. My first extended assignment for them was to provide Black Belt Training. In ideal Black Belt Training, each step of the process improvement methodology is taught over two or three days with the Black Belt assigned a project related to a process in need of improvement. Then, over the course of 4 to 6 weeks, the Black Belt goes off to implement a set of predetermined intersession assignments. During those intersessions, Cedric would meet with each of the teams. I would receive frequent calls asking for advice and input on his thoughts on each project team. When I returned for the formal training, Cedric would ask at the close of each day why I decided to teach the material in a certain way. He not only inquired about the technical material, he would spend considerable time understanding how and why I would teach a certain topic. He quickly learned that a given topic can and should be taught in different ways depending on the audience.

For example, when I taught the overview of Six Sigma to the Lithonia Lighting management, the focus of the benefits was geared toward issues of profitability. Later in the week when I communicated the benefits of Six Sigma to individual contributors at Lithonia, I stressed the greater work-life balance and lower stress working in a more effective and efficient organization. While excellent communication skills cannot necessarily be learned, they can be improved, particularly if the Master Black Belt becomes skilled in knowing what, when, and how to communicate a specific element of Six Sigma.

If possible, the Master Black Belt, like the Quality Leader position, should be hired from within, having the respect of those affected by Six Sigma within the organization, both executives and those involved in the Six Sigma tactical activities.

Another mistake Master Black Belts make is to assume they become better Master Black Belts through greater and greater technical mastery. As Table 5.1 indicates, technical mastery is more than just statistics. While it is important to know statistics as part of their technical skill set, Table 5.1 shows that a Master Black Belt must master management of change and facilitative leadership skills.

Whether it be at the executive level or the project improvement level, change management is a crucial element that contributes to the success of a Six Sigma effort within an organization. Formally or informally, Master Black Belts will be called on to diagnose resistance to Six Sigma and mobilize commitment against resistance. These skills cannot be learned in a textbook. Being exposed to those who exhibit resistance and "learning by doing" is critical to the development of these people skills. I have seen many Master Black Belts who focus on the more statistical tools when, in fact, change management skills are necessary.

Finally, a good Master Black Belt will hone his or her facilitative skills. As we mentioned in *The Six Sigma Revolution,* the major reason project teams fail is their inability to manage team dynamics. Often a project could have been successful if an outside facilitator had been used to help guide the team through some treacherous areas where emotions run high. A Master Black Belt who knows how to set agendas with desired outcomes, methods to achieve results, and the right tool to decide a contentious issue is invaluable. Knowing how to deal with a sensitive issue in a group so that no individual is discounted makes for a greater chance that a project team can be a success. Too often I have seen embittered Master Black Belts who sit in the office hoping their phone will ring with some obscure statistical question when the needs of the Six Sigma team are more cultural in nature.

In yet another example of his multifaceted skills, Cedric Brown personifies the value of a Master Black Belt through his facilitative leadership. Cedric spent several months practicing his facilitative leadership skills after taking my Facilitative

Leadership course. He reported almost an overnight improvement in the effectiveness of team meetings with project improvement teams. This improvement in project team effectiveness caught the attention of executive management which resulted in Cedric being requested to lead a strategic business process meeting. The executives were elated when their meeting was both effective and efficient and this resulted in facilitative leadership becoming standard operating practice within the Lithonia community.

➤ The Black Belt or Green Belt

The Black Belt is the tactical leader of the Process Improvement Team. Black Belts are full-time project leaders with no other responsibility other than to lead three to four teams a year toward progression of team goals through either process improvement (DMAIC) or process design (DMADV). The Green Belt is a part-time position, usually a middle manager who will lead a project or two a year depending on whether a process in their work area is targeted for improvement.

The skill sets of a good Black/Green Belt are more tactical in nature. First and foremost, they must have a firm grasp of the skills referenced in Table 5.1. Their grasp of knowledge does not have to parallel that of a Master Black Belt, yet must be sufficient to lead project team members through the steps in the improvement methodology.

Second, Black/Green Belts must have superb project management skills. While they must have technical knowledge, their organization skills to guide a team through the steps expeditiously is one of the most important talents they must possess. A typical process improvement project can last four to six months. Projects that last more than that are typically unsuccessful. Thus, the Black/Green Belt's project management skills are crucial to the success of the project.

Often overlooked but of equal importance is the Black/ Green Belt's facilitation skills. Teams fail in their efforts if they don't know how to set and follow agendas, allow for preventive activities like ground rules for meetings, and know the difference between a low level intervention (e.g., making eye contact) and high level interventions (e.g, stopping the meeting). Of course, for particularly difficult meetings where the Black/Green Belt may play a more participative role, a call to the Master Black Belt to facilitate is in order.

➤ Team Membership

A common problem in selecting team members is to assume that those are willing and able make the best team members. Many executives who sponsor project improvement teams (called the Team Champion) and the Black Belt/Green Belt are under the impression that team membership should be voluntary. This can be a fatal impression. While it is desirable to have a team member see the benefits of team participation from the start, mobilizing commitment is an added responsibility of the Champion, Black Belt, and even the Master Black Belt if necessary.

Of far greater importance in the selection of team membership is selecting those individuals with the greatest subject matter expertise in the process affected. While data and fact will lead the team to improvement, it cannot be denied that those teams that generate the greatest Six Sigma improvement are those teams with process experts who utilize the Six Sigma concepts and techniques to drive improvement.

Regardless of the initial motivation of team members, the Black/Green Belt will encounter maladaptive behavior. Table 5.2 lists the more common problem behaviors a Black Belt will encounter and lists common methods to address these maladaptive behaviors.

Typical Maladaptive Behaviors	Common Strategies to Address Maladaptive Behaviors
1. *The Know-It-All*—described as a person in the group who feels they know all the answers and the Six Sigma method will just get in their way.	➤ Similar to the individual exhibiting Organizational Resistance, it is important to acknowledge the individual's intelligence and then guide this intelligence into the methods and tools. ➤ Many times it is not what the "know-it-all" knows, but when he or she shares it. Good preventive facilitative behaviors include setting ground rules for the team to operate by. By setting a ground rule of balanced participation, you can usually avoid the impact of this type of personality that can dominate a project team.
2. *No Follow Through*—The type of person who doesn't complete action items.	➤ The root cause of this type of behavior must be determined. In some cases, it is due to the person not understanding the importance of the project and their role in it. Either the Black Belt or Champion needs to create the need for this person. ➤ In other cases, it is poor time management. Helping the person balance his or her workload is the proper corrective action.
3. *The Absent Member*—This type of person is absent from project meetings or one-on-one's with the Black Belt.	➤ Surprisingly, the root cause of this behavior is usually the project team member's manager. If this is the case, the Champion (rather than the Black Belt) should intervene and create the need for this person on the team.

Table 5.2 Common problem behaviors.

Typical Maladaptive Behaviors	Common Strategies to Address Maladaptive Behaviors
4. *The "Yes-But" Person*	➤ "But" is an eraser for everything that comes before it. Thus, the respondent who utters these words is a polite resistor. I recommend the prevention of "keeping an open mind," and then operationalizing this by preventing a sentence starting with the words "but" or "yes, but." ➤ When this behavior is later exhibited, rarely do I have to provide an intervention. Those participants in the room often will "call" the individual using this method to resist.
5. *The "Interruptor"*	➤ Interruptors either need attention or want to redirect a conversation. In the former situation I attempt to allow some leeway with the interruptor, giving them a chance to "show their stuff." In the case of an interruptor redirecting a conversation, I always ask the class for a "process check" to see if the general audience I am talking to wants to move on to another topic.
6. *The Team "Clown"*	➤ I like a joke as much, if not more, as the next person. Dealing with the more tedious elements of project work should call for humor. This type of behavior is not the occasional humorous joke. This is the behavior that attempts to derail the work of the team. As part of a low level intervention, I will not laugh at repeated attempts at being the clown. ➤ For repeated clowning I will ask to talk to the "clown" off line to tone down their humor.

Table 5.2 Continued.

While Table 5.2 is not an exhaustive list of the types of behaviors a Black/Green Belt will encounter among their project teams, it does give a taste of the importance of facilitative
skills needed by a Black Belt other than just the pure technical skills typically associated with the Black or Green Belt.

➤ The Organization's External Consultant

In writing this section, I am aware of the potential to be self-
serving. It has been my good fortune to work with a host of
talented external consultants. With the popularity of Six
Sigma exploding, the demand for quality consultants is overwhelming. Sadly, it is my opinion that the majority of consultants marketing themselves as experts are charlatans at
best. The people I respect in this particular field are a select
group. One reason for this is that true Six Sigma consultants
must have a varied and complex skill set. The list would look
similar to the Master Black Belt discussed earlier in this
chapter (Table 5.1) with one major exception. To truly benefit from hiring an external consultant, you must hire someone with substantial experience. The difficulty here is that
these people are few and far between.

Not only must their experience be substantial, it must be
varied. Many Six Sigma external consultants have years of
experience teaching statistics. Many others have years of experience working with project teams. The type of external
consultant who can benefit your organization has years of
tactical experience *and* strategic experience. Your external
consultant should be able to reference business executives
he or she has worked with to create and help manage the
strategic elements of Six Sigma, not just the training of project teams.

Six Sigma consultants command significant fees. With
the potential for cost savings for the average organization

running into the millions, hiring a Six Sigma consultant can be well worth it. Be wary. Any good Six Sigma consultant will gladly share references with you. Do your homework and check them out. Here are some questions you should ask these references or the consultant:

➤ Which area of Six Sigma (Business Process Management, Project Team Training/Consulting, Change Management, and Facilitative Leadership) is this consultant's strength/weakness?

➤ Do you believe you have achieved a true Six Sigma cultural transformation, achieved cost savings, or failed totally in your effort? To what extent did your external consultant contribute to any of these three areas?

➤ Have you worked with any other consultants and how did this consultant compare favorably or unfavorably to them?

➤ Do you have any plans to bring this consultant back for any consulting in the future?

➤ Was this consultant worth what you paid for him or her?

➤ If there were multiple consultants used from this firm, how significant a "drop-off" was there from the lead consultant to his or her associates?

➤ Did this consultant charge only for on-site time or were calls from his or her office a part of the billable charges? Did they itemize all invoices?

➤ What did this consultant do before they did Six Sigma consulting?

➤ How long have you been a Six Sigma consultant?

➤ What has been the most difficult element in the implementation of Six Sigma at your organization and how did your consultant help/hinder you?

■ HOW TO DEVELOP SIX SIGMA PEOPLE IN YOUR ORGANIZATION

Once your Six Sigma team is on board it is critical to develop not only their talents but also the Six Sigma talents of all employees in your organization. In the first 12 to 18 months of implementation of Six Sigma, two elements of Six Sigma will be visible. First and foremost is the effort put forth by the executive management team to create and sustain the Business Process Management elements discussed in Chapter 2 of *The Six Sigma Revolution*. The other major component is the work of the first series of process improvement teams as they attempt to improve the effectiveness and efficiency of key subprocesses of the organization. This was our focus in Chapters 4 to 9 of *The Six Sigma Revolution*.

Ultimately, however, the concepts of Six Sigma should pervade the entire organization. To do this, people must be trained in both the basic and, in some cases, the advanced elements of Six Sigma. This doesn't mean that massive training should be the first order of business for an organization. However, I like the 52/40 policy some organizations have fostered. This refers to a requirement some organizations have implemented where every person in the organization is required during a calendar year (52 weeks), to take a week's worth (40 hours), of Six Sigma training. The type of training is typically left up to the employee in conjunction with their manager so that their Six Sigma skills are either developed or honed. It is this approach that has resulted in Motorola University, where specific curriculums are created to meet the requirements of the employees.

What are the type of courses that should be offered to the employees? Table 5.1 is the basis for much of the training that should be offered to potential class participants. Common courses that are created in the first year of Six Sigma training include:

Six Sigma Overview	4–8 hours in length
Business Process Management	3 days
Green Belt for Champions	3 or 8 days
Black/Green Belt Training	12 days
Change Management	3 days
Facilitative Management	2 days
Individual Tools Clinic(s)	Depends on the tool or technique

➤ Six Sigma Overview

The commitment to Six Sigma should be a highly publicized event on the part of management. In order for the employees to understand the importance of this change in how the organization will be organized, the Six Sigma Overview is an important first step. Often, not much time or effort is spent on the Six Sigma Overview. This can be a major mistake on the part of the organization. I strongly recommend a four to eight hour overview where management makes a 30- to 45-minute introduction of what led to the organization making the commitment to Six Sigma. This overview should talk about the current financial situation of the organization with emphasis on their competitive threats and cover in general terms the opportunities that await a Six Sigma organization.

It is my suggestion that an external consultant make the remaining presentation. The focus of the remaining presentation should be on the benefits, opportunities, and what is expected of each employee relative to Six Sigma. The reason behind the rationale for the external consultant making the remaining pitch is that in large part the overview is the marketing pitch to the organization. External consultants do this for their living and under normal circumstances an external consultant should be able to "sell" Six Sigma to their general population much as they sold their contract to management. The difficulty of having an internal person making this pitch is that too much time will be spent on the mechanics of Six Sigma. At this point the general employee population will be more interested in how Six Sigma will impact or affect their jobs. Thus, in the hands of a skilled consultant, the key elements of Six Sigma from Business Process Management through to Process Improvement projects should be addressed in the manner that drives the external consultant's marketing acumen.

➤ Business Process Management Training

First and foremost, Six Sigma is a management philosophy. It is only appropriate, therefore, that training begins with management. Unlike other training courses, the Business Process Management training is really a two-part workshop.

Business Process Management is now such a critical element to the final success of Six Sigma, I now insist that all executive management commit to these three days of training before I officially take them on as a client.

In the first two days of this workshop, management creates or reconfirms the strategic business objectives of the organization. Following this, they identify the core, key sub-processes and enabling processes of their organization, followed by identification of who owns the various processes and what the measures of effectiveness and efficiency are for each process. The first two days are finished up by getting a subjective reading of current performance of the effectiveness and efficiency for each process and asking the executives to return in 4 to 6 weeks with actual data of how the processes perform.

Four to six-weeks later, the last day of the workshop is conducted. At this session, the actual data from each process is reviewed, project selection criteria is chosen, the first projects are selected and Champions are chosen.

These three days of training are among the most important an organization undertakes. First, by starting training with management, the clear signal is that, unlike other quality initiatives, management is going to be involved in this one. Second, rather than just a training session per se, management sees actual work being completed. The creation of the Business Process Management System is akin to creating the infrastructure of Six Sigma. Like our highway and turnpike system, it needs upgrading and maintenance. By conducting this training first, management clearly will be sending the message that this is a different approach.

➤ Green Belt for Champions

As indicated, this is either a three- or eight-day process. In the three-day version, once Champions are selected for projects, they go through a business simulation to better understand the DMAIC improvement cycle their teams will embark on in just a few weeks. This business simulation allows Champions to go through three "rounds" of work for a pseudo organization. In Round 1, it is business as usual with chaos, unsatisfied customers, and inefficiency abounding. They learn what Six Sigma is and find out their sigma performance is very poor. They begin to go through the process improvement steps and, during a second round, most teams significantly improve performance. By the second day we round out their learning and allow them an expedited opportunity to take the pseudo organization through improvement with most (but by no means all) Champion teams significantly improving on the first and second round performance.

The eight-day version of Champions training is preferred. This version of Champions training was created in 1997 at GE Capital when Bill Lindenfelder, Beth Galucci, Mike Markovitz, and myself formulated an eight-day training course spread out over two to three months for executives and Champions that forced management to take their own project to completion utilizing the DMAIC and Change Management elements for a project on a smaller level than the first project teams. Ultimately, this course ended up being the highest rated course in the Six Sigma curriculum for GE Capital. By taking their own project from start to finish, Champions developed a much keener sense of how to guide someone else's project once larger scale projects were chartered.

Whether it is the three or eight-day version, training Champions prior to Process Improvement projects is a critical success factor to the overall success of an organization's Six Sigma effort. One element in the success of Six Sigma at the tactical level is the active involvement of Champions. In the beginning of a Six Sigma launch, Champions "don't know what they don't know." Getting them to know how to guide a team through the steps of either Process Improvement or Process Design doesn't happen by chance.

■ BLACK/GREEN BELT TRAINING

At Eckes and Associates, Inc., we believe once the infrastructure is created and Champions are trained in their responsibilities, project training is scheduled. A key element of this training is having projects selected from the last day of Business Process Management training that have high impact to the business objectives of the organization that also are currently performing at poor sigma levels.

Black/Green Belt training is based on "action learning." This concept says that people learn best by applying new tools and techniques to actual work in their area. Thus, the Black/Green Belt training should be divided up into the DMAIC elements with just-in-time training for each segment of the Process Improvement milestone once their projects have been determined by the project Champion. Usually I and one of my associates train the Define and Measurement modules in the following manner:

> ## Day 1 – Define

>   > We begin with an overview of Business Process Management and discuss with the project teams the ongoing work of the executive team. This usually boosts commitment to the project team's morale as they see that their work is not created in a vacuum. Recognition that executive management is in the process of creating and sustaining the Six Sigma infrastructure

increases employee morale toward their tactical project responsibilities around Six Sigma.

➤ We review the major elements of the first of the three major milestones of the Define step in process improvement—the Team Charter. Included in the lecture is reconfirmation of the business case for the team project. A good business case usually links the work of the project team with the strategic business objectives of the organization.

➤ We help the team craft a preliminary problem statement. This problem statement should describe how long the problem has existed, describe the gap between current and desired performance, indicate the impact the problem is having and be stated in neutral terms so that no one on the problem team is jumping to predetermined causes or solutions and no blame is attributable.

➤ The team is taught the importance of *project scope.* Scope refers to the boundaries under which the team operates. They should be guided by the thoughts of the project Champion about what they should work on and more importantly, what they *shouldn't* be working on. However skilled the project team's Champion is, my associate or I ask the project team during a breakout activity to provide their thoughts on project scope and validate their thoughts with the project Champion during the intersession.

➤ We review the various roles and responsibilities of the team from the Champion to the Master Black Belt and

Black/Green Belt. We allow break-out time for the Black or Green Belts to review and revise team responsibilities based on what they hear during our lecture.

➤ Finally, we talk about the milestones for their project and what they must do in their leadership role relative to project management. We stress the importance of projects being brought to fruition in 120 to 160 days and allow time during a break-out for the Black/Green Belt to address logistical issues with project planning.

➤ Day 2—Define

➤ The second major milestone of the Define step of DMAIC is the determination of who the customer(s) of the project is, what they need from the process, and the requirements of the customer(s). During this lecture, we introduce methods in how to determine who the customer(s) are, whether it is important to segment the customer population, and how to obtain information on the customer(s) requirements. During the break-out activity for this section of the course, we allow the project teams to brainstorm about who the customer(s) of the project are, their needs and requirements, stressing to the team that this work needs to be validated during the intersession.

➤ The last milestone of the Define stage of the project is to create a high-level Process Map of the process to be improved. The mnenomic device called SIPOC helps the team create this high-level map—supplier, inputs, process, outputs, and customer. We stress the importance that what the team creates in break-out session must be validated before they return for the next session.

➤ Intersession

At the close of the second day of training, my associate or I task the project teams on what they need to do before we return for Measurement training. We stress the importance of meeting with the project Champion within the first week after this training to confirm all elements of the charter before going further. We indicate that all customers, and their needs and requirements must be validated. Finally, we indicate that the Process Map created during the second day of training must be validated before their return for Measurement training.

Typically, approximately six weeks are allowed for this intersession work, sometimes more and sometimes less. We emphasize to each Black/Green Belt that the degree to which intersession work is completed is a critical success factor toward achievement of the project goals. We indicate that upon our return each Black/Green Belt will give a 15- to 30-minute status report on what they accomplished in the intersession.

➤ Day 3 and 4—Measurement

➤ The morning of our return we hear project status reports. We invite the Champions to attend this session and hear how both their team and the other teams are progressing.

➤ At the onset of the day we show the data collection plan and the eight columns that need to be filled out for baseline sigma to ultimately be calculated. The first column indicates what is to be measured. These need to be the most important measures of the current level of effectiveness and efficiency in the process targeted for improvement. The second column is whether the measurement is an output measure (a measure of effectiveness in the eyes of the customer), an input measure (a measure of supplier effectiveness), or a process measure (a measure of the efficiency of how the process operates).

In the third column, we teach that there are two basic ways to collect measures, using either discrete or continuous data. The former is binary data; good/bad, on/off, and so on. Continuous data is data collected on a continuum, like weight, height, time, and so on.

In the fourth column, we ask each team to operationally define their measures. Operational definitions refer to how consistently the data will be collected. This step is crucial for the ultimate data to be respected and accepted by the customer. For example, at GE Aircraft Engine they have a concept called "Wing to Wing." Initially, a Six Sigma project team attempting to improve timeliness of engine maintenance would measure the time the engine was in the maintenance area while the engine was actually being repaired. However, the customer measured timeliness as the time the engine was removed from the aircraft wing to the time it was put back on the aircraft wing. This crucial difference in operational definitions made for significant variation in the sigma performance. We teach each of our teams to operationalize their measures as the customer would.

Typically at this time we have yet another break-out and the project teams begin creating the first four columns of the all-important data collection plan.

➤ Upon completion, the first four columns are reported on, then we continue in lecture with review of data collection forms, how to sample, and how to calculate baseline sigma. (For details on these elements of Six Sigma, refer to *The Six Sigma Revolution*.)

➤ Intersession

At the close of the fourth day of training, we once again define what each team needs to do relative to the "Measure" element of DMAIC. We stress the importance of creating the data collection plan and implementing the plan, so that upon our return six to eight weeks later, the teams return with baseline sigma performance on their projects.

➤ Day 5 and 6 — Analysis

➤ As always, upon our return the first morning of training is devoted to project reviews (with Champions invited) to see how their team and other teams are progressing. After each report, each team is provided with positive feedback and suggestions for improvement.

➤ In the Analysis phase, we describe how to take data that has been collected and analyze potential patterns or clues that drive current sigma performance. We then teach teams to conduct process analysis and to examine and record current inefficiencies.

➤ Whether through data analysis or process analysis (or, more likely, a combination of both), the team will learn how to formulate more specific problem statements than originally created in the Define stage of the project.

➤ At this point, we turn to one of the most important elements in a Six Sigma team's work, determining the root causes for current Six Sigma performance. It is this area that teams often skim over, anxious to get to their improvement suggestions which may lack the data that drive true sigma performance. We teach methods to determine and verify root causation and give teams break-out time to begin this important stage of the project.

➤ Intersession

This third intersession period is critical to the team's success. We stress at the close of Day 6 training that validation of the root causes brainstormed during the training is one of the most important factors associated with the success of projects. For some teams, the use of designed experiments as a way to validate root causation requires an additional three days of training which takes place during the intersession.

➤ Day 7, 8, and 9—Improve

➤ As always, we begin with a review of projects with particular attention paid to whether teams have used data to verify root causes.

➤ With evidence of root causation established, project teams are ready to learn how to develop the improvement suggestions that will increase baseline sigma performance. This section of the course is divided into two major areas. First, the technical solutions that will drive sigma improvement. Second, how to gain acceptance of those solutions, the latter of which uses many of the tools referenced in this book.

➤ Intersession

In the four to six weeks of intersession, the project team formulates their solutions and develops a plan for implementation. We strongly suggest that the team pilot their solutions on a small scale during the intersession. Most of the intersession should be focused on development of acceptance of solutions. In many cases, actual improvement will take much longer than the intersession.

➤ Day 10 and 11 — Improve and Control

➤ In this last session, we begin as always with reports. In some cases, improvement is reported at this time. In these final days of training, we cover two remaining issues. First, we address the technical areas of how to control the process and sustain improved sigma performance. Second, we address how to create a reponse plan for how the new process will be operated once the project team disbands. During this session, we strongly recommend that the project Champion and Process Owner be present to completely understand how the new process will sustain improved sigma performance.

Particularly if this is the first wave of Black Belt training, we encourage the organization to have a combination science fair and celebratory awards banquet. Recognition and reward for both effort and results are beneficial for both the first wave of Black/Green Belts as well as for future Black/Green Belts.

■ CHANGE MANAGEMENT

Eckes and Associates, Inc. strongly suggests to its clients that they adopt change management as part of their Six Sigma curriculum. Change management can be taught two ways. In the first change management course, acceptance of Six Sigma at the strategic level is addressed. Our earlier chapters on creating the need, shaping the vision, and mobilizing commitment to Six Sigma within an organization are just three examples of strategic change management education.

In the other change management course, the same tools referenced above are taught to project teams to gain better acceptance of the proposed solutions for their project.

■ FACILITATIVE MANAGEMENT

Another course not typically a part of a Six Sigma curriculum is facilitative management. At the project level, many teams fail because of poor team dynamics, such as poor or nonexistent agendas, no desired outcomes for when the team meets, no operating agreements for team behaviors, and no method to address inappropriate team behaviors. At the same time, if the goal of Six Sigma is to improve the effectiveness and efficiency of an organization, facilitative skills can dramatically improve the efficiency of an organization whether the focus is project improvement teams or meetings in general.

Jack Becker at Lithonia Lighting calculated that reducing inefficiencies in his organization during meetings would be equivalent to an additional 10 percent improvement in productivity without the cost of hiring new personnel.

■ INDIVIDUAL TOOLS CLINIC(S)

There will be instances in which project teams, Master Black Belts, Black/Green Belts, and executives within an organization will be faced with the need for tool-specific training. For example, Design of Experiments (DOE) is a potent tool that some teams will need to apply to their projects if they are to validate root causation and assist in determining sigma improvement factors.

While an important tool, not all teams will need to use Design of Experiments. Thus, DOE training should be on a need-to-know basis. At Eckes and Associates, DOE is one of our favorite tools and one of the more popular stand-alone seminars we sponsor. I would never assume that this tool need be taught every time in the Analysis section of the course. Six Sigma consultants need to practice what they preach. The training a Black Belt needs to go through to successfully lead a project team is daunting enough without introducing tools that may or may not be used.

A good consultant or Master Black Belt will recognize that a subgoal of any good training class is increasing both the interest and confidence in those attending the course, not "showing off" what the instructor knows. I have attended too many training sessions on Six Sigma where the apparent goal of the class is to show how much the consultant knows rather than increase the competency and confidence of the attendees.

There are a host of other tools and techniques far too numerous to mention by name. A tools clinic approach to training will meet the needs and requirements of the organization rather than the massive tool infusion training known by some in the trade as "sheep dipping."

While class participants need something to reference, also be careful of the psychological overload of handing out a workbook containing tools that will not be covered in the seminar. One mistake that GE Capital made in their training materials was putting together a workbook that was literally hundreds of pages long for improvement teams and Black Belt training. Already feeling like they are visiting a dentist at the beginning of the seminar, many participants would see me unloading book binders (some of which were so stuffed they had broken some of the rings in the binder themselves) and begin to bemoan what awaited them even though I pledged not to cover every page.

■ HOW TO EVALUATE PERSONNEL IN YOUR ORGANIZATION RELATIVE TO SIX SIGMA

The adage "what gets measured gets done," applies to how personnel should be evaluated in Six Sigma. Jack Welch introduced this paradigm shown in Figure 5.1, at General Electric even before Six Sigma became their predominant management philosophy. He believed that both achieving results and embracing the values of the organization were critical if the goals and objectives of the organization were to be achieved. Figure 5.1 shows the four quadrants in a matrix where the vertical axis are results and the horizontal axis are the values. In this discussion, the values to be embraced are the Six Sigma values and behaviors we referenced in Chapter 3.

Ultimately we want our personnel (particularly management) to be in the upper right-hand quadrant. Those that achieve high results and are high performers in terms of the values and behaviors of Six Sigma are those performers targeted for promotion.

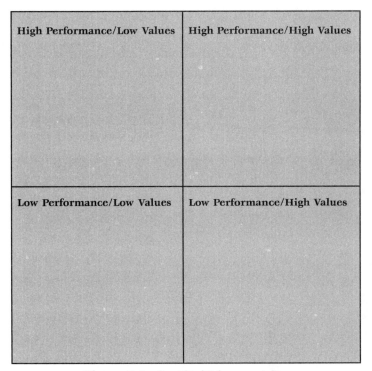

Figure 5.1 Results/Values matrix.

There will be those who are high achievers with low performance in terms of Six Sigma values and behaviors. At General Electric, Jack Welch believes these performers need to be coached in the values and beliefs, thinking that performance can be even further enhanced through adhering to such tenets as Six Sigma.

There are some who embrace these values and beliefs but whose performance isn't what it should be. More than one manager has embraced Six Sigma thinking that it would save his job rather than seeing Six Sigma as an enabler toward better performance. These individuals need to be coached but perhaps with a shorter rein and time element than the high performer/low values individual.

Little need be said for the lower left-hand quadrant individual. These people need to be ushered out the door before their negativeness pervades the entire organization. As Jack Welch has repeatedly said, too many organizations spend too much time on their C employees when they need to be working on turning their B employees into A employees and rewarding and recognizing their A employees.

In evaluating Six Sigma performance, there is the assumption that current performance is being measured. I have found that this assumption is not always a safe one to make. The importance of performance measurement regardless of whether you practice Six Sigma or not cannot be overstated.

Any time I conduct a seminar, facilitate a project meeting, or coordinate the creation of a process management system with senior management, I always begin the day with a set of introductions, establish ground rules, and share statements of the participants of their desired outcomes for our time together. Then, at the end of each day, I request that the participants anonymously fill out and post on a flip chart the "Pluses" and the "Deltas" (what could have been different) of the day.

Although having been a consultant for nearly 20 years has taught me what works well with an audience and what doesn't work well, I pride myself on always studying the pluses and deltas. The plus/delta daily feedback and the overall seminar evaluations I have received from clients continuously reshapes the overall delivery of my material.

Remember my adage about feedback: "Feedback is a gift. Some gifts can be returned." The first time I said those words I was speaking to Meg Hartzler, cofounder and principal consultant for the Destra Consulting Firm. Meg was quick to point out the Hartzler response to my premise: "Yes, some gifts can be returned, but if you return all your gifts, after a while you won't get any more gifts."

Meg's comment hit home with me back in the early 1990s when I first heard it. I have attempted religiously to first find out what my customer's requirements are for any training or consulting I do for them and then collect data to determine how well I have done against those requirements.

Sometimes I don't like the gifts I receive. Some gifts are returned, if ever so silently. However, I am a firm believer that some type of data collection relative to individual performance against Six Sigma expectations are an important element in the acceptance of Six Sigma in an organization.

To evaluate performance means there is a set of clear objectives and expectations to measure against. I will attempt to answer what should be in the objectives in two ways. First, the tactical elements against which any person should be evaluated in terms of Six Sigma implementation; and second, how to incorporate the spirit of Six Sigma in performance reviews.

Tactically, what an employee should be evaluated against relative to Six Sigma is dependent on where in the organization the employee is. We will address three areas of an organization:

1. Upper management

2. Quality personnel

3. Individual contributors

➤ Upper Management

At General Electric, Jack Welch stated early in their Six Sigma implementation that managers who qualified for a bonus would have 40 percent of that bonus dependent on their Six Sigma involvement.

In the early stages of Six Sigma implementation at General Electric, the 40 percent involvement was vaguely defined. Involvement for management included:

➤ Creation of the Business Process Management System, specifically helping define the strategic business objectives of the organization, determining the core/key sub/enabling processes of the organization, establishing process measurements, determining project selection criteria and using the criteria to select high impact projects.

➤ When appropriate, assisting in the DMAIC improvement methodology. Specifically, selecting potential Black and Green Belts. When appropriate, being a Champion to project teams that affect processes in their area. This would include creating the business case for the project, selecting team members, providing the strategic direction for the project, removing barriers to the potential success of the project, acting as the formal liason between the project team and the executive team, rewarding and recognizing the project team, and institutionalizing the success of the project team.

➤ Assisting in the management of change relative to Six Sigma. Specifically, assisting in creating the need for Six Sigma in the organization, assisting in shaping the Six Sigma vision/results/behaviors of Six Sigma, helping to overcome resistance to Six Sigma, and assisting in changing the necessary systems and structures for Six Sigma to thrive within the organization.

➤ Participation in all pertinent training and education.

➤ Involvement in the Business Quality Council.

➤ Quality Personnel

Invariably, business organizations soon recognize the importance of including quality personnel in their bonus programs (see the compensation section later in this chapter). Whether a Quality Leader, Master Black Belt, or Key Black Belt, the bonus eligibility should be based on the following:

➤ Quality Leaders should be evaluated on how well they help shape the strategic elements of Six Sigma. This specifically should address the creation and maintenance of the Business Process Management System. The maintenance of the Six Sigma effort is based on the quantity and quality of the business quality council meetings that eventually should be the executive staff's only formal meeting time. In addition, Quality Leaders should be evaluated tactically on project results.

➤ For Master Black Belts and Key Black Belts, evaluation should be based on technical knowledge, training ability, project results, and requests of the Master Black Belt or Key Black Belt from selected teams and/or management.

➤ Individual Contributors

The majority of any organization's employees will not be a part of a bonus program. Instead, a part of their individual performance review should include specific tactical expectations around Six Sigma. Specifically, they should include:

➤ Participation in project teams when requested.

➤ Acceptance of the role of Process Owner, if applicable.

➤ Acceptance of the role of project Champion, if applicable.

➤ Attendance at all necessary training.

➤ Implementation of the control plans for other project team's work if they are affected by the plan to either implement solutions or control the process after improvement.

In addition to the aforementioned tactical elements that all employees should be evaluated on relative to Six Sigma, performance reviews should be used to capture the spirit of Six Sigma within an organization.

In the November 1994 *Quality Progress* magazine (pp. 57–60), I wrote about practical alternatives to performance appraisals. As organizations move to more process-oriented structures, performance appraisals need to be modified to capture how well employees satisfy the needs and requirements of customers, whether those customers are external to the organization or internal to the organization. As part of a restructuring of performance appraisals, I recommend organizations go through five steps:

1. *Identify customers.* For any department, function, or employee, customers should be identified and stratified into three categories (remember we define a customer as the recipient of our products and/or services). The first of those categories is the external customers of the employee in question. The second stratification should be the internal interdepartmental

customers who exist within the organization. Finally, customers considered intradepartmental should be identified. In this last category, many organizations see the manager as a supplier of services and the employees in that department are considered the customer of managerial services.

2. *Identify customer requirements.* In the case of identifying the manager as supplier, it would then be expected for the manager to identify the requirements of his or her employees. One list totaling almost 50 was narrowed down to the four most important requirements:
   —Accessibility
   —Leadership
   —Participative management
   —Conduct effective/efficient performance reviews

3. *Determine metrics for current performance.* A rating scale was created where each supplier rated the manager on the four requirements. An example of the scale is:
   (1) The supplier does not meet requirements.
   (2) The supplier meets requirements but needs development.
   (3) The supplier meets requirements and exceeds them at times.
   (4) The supplier consistently exceeds requirements.

4. *Data is collected and improvement opportunities identified.* Once requirements are identified and metrics for performance are determined, data is collected. Whether the client is external, interdepartmental, or intradepartmental, customers are solicited to determine how well the supplier of products or services is doing the job. In the above managerial example, every

90 days the manager is reviewed by his or her employees. A score of 2 or 1 means that step five must be completed.

5. *Improvement plans created and implemented.* For deficient evaluations, corrective action on the part of the supplier is required and evaluated at the time of the next data collection.

In these five steps, the spirit of being customer-focused is captured formally as part of everyone's performance appraisal. When organizations begin to recognize that only when they require customer focus as a documented way of doing business will their organizations start to embrace Six Sigma.

■ HOW TO REWARD AND RECOGNIZE PERSONNEL IN YOUR ORGANIZATION RELATIVE TO SIX SIGMA

In my years of being a practicing psychologist, I learned many concepts that have influenced both my later professional life and even my personal life. As mentioned earlier, during my last full year as a practicing psychologist, I spent some time doing marital therapy. One pattern among unhappy couples I quickly observed was their tendency to find fault with the other party. When this was brought to their attention, the accuser was quick to defend his or her accusations, including data to support the negative behavior they were "catching" their spouse engaged in. This type of behavior seemed to impel the other spouse to do the exact same thing.

At this time I was living in Bowling Green, Ohio, attending classes at Bowling Green State University to obtain an

MBA with the ultimate goal of getting into the business world. Among my circle of friends were two professors who taught in the business school who had been married to one another for close to 25 years. It was my impression that this couple was happily married. At first I was skeptical with their apparent happiness, thinking it was an act for a new acquaintance. As time passed and we developed a closer friendship, I became truly amazed at the level of true intimacy and respect each of the two had for one another. Finally, over dinner one day I asked what the secret was to their happiness.

"One simple rule," they told me, "always catch your spouse doing something *right*."

What a profound impact this simple axiom has had on my life. If management wants Six Sigma to be more than a passing fad in their organization, they need to practice this simple rule.

In the last few pages we discussed how various levels within an organization should be evaluated in an organization. We now discuss how employees and groups should be rewarded and recognized to further propel the Six Sigma culture. First we discuss management, then discuss how to reward and recognize Six Sigma quality professionals, then finish with how to reward and recognize project improvement teams.

➤ Rewarding and Recognizing Management

The traditional difference between reward and recognition is that the former is financially oriented while recognition is typically a nonfinancial incentive. We earlier talked about how General Electric created the incentive for management to embrace Six Sigma through management bonuses. This is the typical incentive created for management. The 40 percent of the management bonus tied to Six Sigma is an aggressive incentive that will capture and motivate management.

➤ Rewarding and Recognizing Quality Professionals

The Quality Leader is considered part of the management group and their reward and recognition should be no more or less than any other executive. My comments here are directed more to the Master Black Belt. As we discussed earlier, the Master Black Belt can play a pivotal role in the success of both the tactical and strategic elements of the Six Sigma effort. Many of the organizations I have consulted with have learned in a very painful way that failure to adequately compensate a high-performing Master Black Belt can result in the loss of a significant investment.

One client that had one of the better Master Black Belts I had encountered compensated her with pay only slightly above a Black Belt and without access to the bonus pool or stock options. She indicated to her Quality Leader her worth to the organization and her dissatisfaction with her compensation. Nothing but future promises were given and soon this Master Black Belt left the organization.

Therein lies the problem for an organization attempting to keep their better Master Black Belts. The Master Black Belt is equivalent to an external consultant if they become good enough. Thus, I encourage a creative package of reward and recognition for a Master Black Belt. First, provide them with a base pay in the low six figures. If this seems high for your organization, remember the average cost savings for a typical project is $175,000. Knowing the Master Black Belt will play a significant role in most projects, a base pay in the low six figures is very reasonable. Second, include your better Master Black Belts in your bonus pool and/or stock options program. Finally, I have worked out with selected clients what I believe is a "Win-Win" strategy. In several cases where I became aware of the Master Black Belt being coveted by consulting companies, I offered both my client and the Master Black Belt the opportunity to have the Master Black Belt be my associate on an extremely limited basis. This is usually done during the Master Black Belt's vacation or unpaid leave time. Recognizing the opportunity costs of having to retrain a new Master Black Belt and the impact this type of departure would have on your business should lead the organization to create a creative compensation, reward, and recognition program.

➤ Reward and Recognition of Your Black Belt and Project Teams

When it comes to the reward and recognition of Black Belts and Project teams, most consultants will advise you to provide token reward and recognition. I have seen teams rewarded with gift certificates, pizza parties, plaques, or T-shirts.

In one case, I happened to be doing a Train the Trainer program for a group of Master Black Belts. A prominent automobile manufacturer had worked with another consultant on Black Belt training and at the time of my arrival they had several high-profile success stories. Their interest in hiring me was to develop their Master Black Belts sufficient to provide future training, an element of consulting we specialize in. On the second day of training with their Master Black Belts, their CEO had called for a special recognition and rewards luncheon.

I had been requested to halt the training of their Master Black Belts for them to attend the luncheon because one of the DMAIC projects was to be recognized at the meeting. The

CEO grandly went through a five-minute recitation of how the project team dramatically improved a key process of the business and in the process saved close to one million dollars. The reaction was highly positive, at least initially. The team virtually blushed as they received the recognition of peers and superiors in the room.

Then something happened that strongly influenced me against using only recognition of project teams. Just after the recognition of the project team, the CEO went on to identify the best nonmanager performer for the year. The winner of this yearly award was granted the use of an upscale, $50,000 automobile where their only financial responsibility was fuel. Insurance and maintenance were provided along with the use of the car.

As the CEO described why this person was selected, my heart sank. The CEO spent nearly 10 minutes detailing how this individual had dealt with an international car dealer, working on weekends and evenings, supplanting his vacation to provide this dealer with product. Great, this organization had verbally committed to Six Sigma and had recognized a project team. However, their hearts and minds were committed to rewarding the "fire-fighter" while giving only token recognition to the less glamorous role of those who fought to find and arrest the arsonist. I knew at that moment that this organization wasn't going to become a Six Sigma cultural success story. I quickly completed my contract and did not return to this client.

This also brings me to my strong recommendation for how to reward and recognize Black Belt and project teams. I strongly recommend gain sharing. In gain sharing, a successful project team's success is quantified financially. Let's say a project team generates $450,000 in cost savings. Gain sharing would be when a certain percentage (maybe 5 percent for the entire team) of the $450,000 would be distributed back to the team that generated the cost savings. A $450,000 cost savings would mean $22,500 would be split among the 5 to 8 team members and the Black Belt. While the vast majority of the cost savings would be the organizations, knowing each individual will share in the profits will generate tremendous enthusiasm and greater results associated with projects.

I have not been advocating this approach for long but initial reaction tends to reveal how popular this approach can be. In recent seminars, I have begun collecting informal data. I ask nonmanagers which of the following they prefer, reward or recognition. In each of the cases, the overwhelming response is that reward is preferred over recognition.

It is my belief that a major source of lower level resistance to Six Sigma could be dramatically reduced if this gainsharing approach was adopted for Black Belts and project teams. I would further propose that there are ways to reduce, if not eliminate, the potential for any abuse. As part of the Business Quality Council I referenced in Chapter 9 of *The Six Sigma Revolution,* I would recommend a review board made up of front-line workers who have already participated in improvement projects, Master Black Belts, the financial analysts of the organization, and selected management. It would be this committee who would review and report on the actual cost savings for each successful project. In this way, there would be both accountability and greater interest among projects that would benefit all involved.

■ HOW TO COMMUNICATE SIX SIGMA IN YOUR ORGANIZATION

The general employee population will be skeptical when they first become aware that their organization is attempting to embrace this popular management philosophy. In all likelihood, the organization has made some previous attempt at productivity improvement and in all likelihood that effort failed. One area that probably contributed to previous failures is poor communication of Six Sigma. When any change is successful, those driving the change must communicate the change on various levels. In this section, I address several of the more important venues where Six Sigma needs to be communicated.

Specific communication venues I have seen contribute to Six Sigma success include:

➤ The Six Sigma kick-off.

➤ Six Sigma communication to the financial community.

➤ Six Sigma and managers meetings.

➤ Six Sigma as the first thing on your agenda.

➤ Six Sigma as a secondary marketing strategy.

➤ Six Sigma and your suppliers.

➤ Six Sigma success story circulation.

➤ The Business Quality Council.

➤ The Six Sigma Kick-Off

Many organizations minimize the importance of the Six Sigma kick-off meeting. You only have one chance to make a good first impression. As such, the kick-off meeting needs to accomplish several goals. The first 30 to 45 minutes should be done by the highest ranking executive in the organization. In his or her remarks, they need to briefly describe the series of events that have led the organization to embracing Six Sigma. In some instances, the executive will be describing a "burning platform." A burning platform is based on imagining some burning oil rig in the ocean, where, despite the need for land, the riggers need to take the plunge into the cold waters. This metaphor is used to describe some threat, external or internal, that prompts the organization to change the way they do business.

During the kick-off meeting, the executive needs to explain this "burning platform" in easy-to-understand language to create the need for Six Sigma. Using the approach we described in Chapter 2, it is important for the executive to have the proof necessary to show to his or her audience why the move to Six Sigma was needed. The case study I used in Chapter 2 of *The Six Sigma Revolution* where the Westin Tabor Center was threatened with loss of their four-star hotel rating as their reason for pursuing Business Process Management is a clear and documented "burning platform" example.

Clearly this approach would not have worked if Jack Welch had tried to show a "burning platform" for General Electric. There would have been no proof to show his point. Instead, Jack Welch talked in his kick-off to Six Sigma about taking General Electric to the next level. In the mid-1990s, he talked about the world-class organization he wanted General Electric to be in 2001.

Regardless of the approach in the first minutes of the kick-off, it is critical that the need for Six Sigma be created in clear, concise language by the business leader.

It is recommended that an external consultant then present an overview of Six Sigma. The consultant should address the major components of Six Sigma. First, there should be an overview of the Business Process Management elements that the executive team will be creating and managing. I usually discuss Business Process Management through sharing a case study and highlighting the eight steps to its creation. I give a status of where the host organization is in its implementation strategy. This allows the audience to see that, unlike most other efforts, this one is different. Unlike other efforts this organization has attempted, management will play an active role. This creates a greater sense of believability in Six Sigma on the part of the audience. If management is serious enough about Six Sigma to actively participate, then this must be a true commitment. I then focus on the DMAIC improvement methodology, again sharing a case study of an actual client who has successfully moved through the five improvement steps.

In addition to creating the need for Six Sigma and showing that this initiative is different from past efforts, the final goal of the Six Sigma overview is to express expectations. These expectations need to be specific and time-related. Remember the first rule of change is resistance to anything new. This produces anxiety. This anxiety can be reduced if specific expectations are stated. For example, some of those in the kick-off audience might be a part of the first wave of DMAIC improvement projects. If so, review the tentative schedule of training and what will be expected over the course of the training. It is also possible that the audience may not be involved in specific involvement for months to come. If so, stating this explicitly can assuage fears and anxieties.

➤ Six Sigma Communication to the Financial Community

I have worked with Lipper Analytical, an organization that reviews various mutual funds. A part of their work is attending financial reviews of various businesses. I was once told that even before General Electric had generated results in their Six Sigma effort, their stock price favorably improved because of the successful communication of their commitment to Six Sigma.

If your organization is of interest to Wall Street, don't ignore including your commitment to Six Sigma in your updates. It will undoubtedly have a positive impact on your stock price. Furthermore, this communication is a public pronouncement which cannot easily be reversed. This, in part, may explain why Wall Street favorably sees the pronouncement as a long-term commitment to improvement. The later abandonment of Six Sigma would be far more negatively perceived than never committing to Six Sigma in the first place.

➤ Six Sigma and Managers' Meetings

Once an organization commits to a Six Sigma initiative, management must use any and all communication vehicles to show their unwavering commitment to Six Sigma and provide status on its progress. I have advised executives to place Six Sigma updates on any agenda where they are present.

Most organizations have an all-managers' meeting where the business leader provides a status on the events impacting the business. I recommend that business leaders include Six Sigma and to profile Six Sigma prominently. Do not place the Six Sigma item at the end, but much earlier in the agenda. This accomplishes two things: First, items toward the end of the agenda are often modified or edited out altogether. Put Six Sigma there and it sends the message that Six Sigma is something to be done after everything else. Put it earlier in the agenda and the business leader sends the message that this is important. Second, by putting it earlier in the agenda it forces the business leader to do the prework to say something important about Six Sigma.

These all-managers' meetings are important to the business leader and they put some prework into their comments. By having Six Sigma earlier in the agenda not only do they have to think about Six Sigma more, it also leads to them spending more time working on Six Sigma.

➤ Six Sigma as the First Thing on Your Agenda

Traveling as much as I do can wreck havoc on your parenting abilities. Knowing this, I have diligently attempted to create structure with my two boys through my communication on the road. I always ask what homework they are working on, what they are reading, and what the highlight and lowlight was for their day. By doing this, I have established an expectation.

You can do this in your organization. An expectation should be that each manager not only include Six Sigma as part of his or her agenda, but have it be one of the first items on the agenda. This will force the manager to do prework and more actively involve themselves in Six Sigma.

In addition, it will gradually lead to Six Sigma being a part of the organization's culture. There is a story told about Bob Galvin, the former CEO of Motorola, who was the first business leader to champion Six Sigma. In 1992, we were both speakers at the Annual Juran Institute. He was the keynote speaker and I was giving a tutorial on supplier management. We had a brief time to talk during the speaker's hospitality session. I asked him about a rumor I had heard during the 1980s that he would request that staff meetings begin with an update on Six Sigma implementation and then he would leave. He indicated that he had done that. Moreover, he gave a great reason for it. The reason wasn't just to stress the importance of Six Sigma implementation. It also forced his executives to communicate normal business practices using the Six Sigma methodology. This last point really stuck with me. If the financial officer wanted to communicate financial updates, he had to talk the language of Business Process Management (i.e., dashboards). Another of my clients took my advice to start each all-managers' meeting with a Six Sigma update. Soon, he found himself talking the language of Business Process Management—process dashboards and balanced scorecards—in a way that made Six Sigma a "way of doing business," not something he did in his spare time.

➤ Six Sigma as a Secondary Marketing Strategy

I don't recommend this as a beginning communication method. There is a tendency for the sales and marketing group to be among the last disciplines to move to a more supportive role in the Six Sigma roll-out, while there are exceptions to this (most notably Mike Delaney at Unifi Textiles). I stress to the sales and marketing function how many organizations ultimately use their Six Sigma initiative as a secondary marketing strategy.

In the 1980s, one computer company I worked with quickly learned that the successes they were experiencing in their quality effort soon became a secondary marketing strategy. Customers and potential customers can be seduced into seeing the beauty of *someone else's* successful efforts. It all looks so easy from afar. In more than one case, the Six Sigma success stories and the offer to jump-start the customer's Six

Sigma effort can lead the sales and marketing group to see Six Sigma as a potent tool to help find and keep potential customers.

At Compunet, a German information processing firm located in Frankfurt, they have communicated their Six Sigma success and now assist customers in their Six Sigma efforts. In the fall of 1999, Eckes and Associates, Inc. kicked off a Six Sigma effort with one of Compunet's customers in Madrid. These efforts not only strengthened the relationship between customer and supplier, it has the potential to assist further business transactions between supplier and customer.

➤ Six Sigma and Your Suppliers

Communication about your Six Sigma initiative should also be directed toward and with suppliers. In the last 20 years, the perspective of the supplier as a necessary evil has changed dramatically. The concept of Supplier Management has turned the supplier into a partner. Six Sigma communication is a tangible way to strengthen the partnering concept.

An earlier example I used was a computer company who had an incoming reject rate averaging in the mid-teens. At this point, a receiving inspection group would either sort good from bad product and send the remaining parts to the production line or reject the shipped lot and require the supplier to resend a better one. With such a high reject rate, suppliers were seen as a necessary evil and often were blamed for production or reliability problems. Through a supplier quality assistance group, we began communicating the quality initiative (close but not identical to Motorola's Six Sigma approach at the time) to the 900+ suppliers located worldwide.

In a series of cluster seminars to communicate our new quality expectations of suppliers, I vividly remember a presentation at the Indianapolis Airport Holiday Inn. The Vice President of Manufacturing and I were making a communications presentation to a select group of suppliers geographically located in that area. In the middle of the first morning session, a self-made millionaire owner of a casting manufacturing firm who had driven up from Cincinnati proclaimed our quality effort a sham and got up and left. Clearly, this supplier had experienced difficulty with my client in the past. Later I learned that this supplier had assisted in the design of new parts for the client with the understanding he would later be chosen as the primary supplier for the part. That didn't happen; the contract went to a competitor.

Why am I telling you of this supplier? Because in less than two years what we first communicated to him in Indianapolis became a reality. If the supplier had stayed around that day in 1984 he would have learned that my client wanted to partner with each supplier, including those who were experiencing quality problems. An offer to the suppliers was communicated that day in Indianapolis. Ironically, less than two years later this supplier became one of my clients' greatest success story. In 1986, this casting owner was experiencing massive quality problems with the surface finish of a milled aluminum casting that served as the deck for a reel-to-reel tape drive. Reluctantly, and obviously desperate, the supplier agreed for me and my staff to come to Cincinnati and work a DMAIC type project heavily using designed experiments to improve their milling process. The results were amazing. The key parameter in question, the microfinish of the casting, was improved over 75 percent and a subsequent hand-polishing process downstream from the milling process was totally eliminated. As a result, an annual cost savings of over $100,000 was actualized making this a win-win for both supplier and customer.

My client then used this success and others like it to communicate the new approach to their supplier management process. Be aware of how your Six Sigma initiative can be used as a way to communicate a changed philosophy of how you manage your supplier base.

➤ Six Sigma Successes through Your Intranet

The growing use of the intranet is yet another venue to communicate Six Sigma through your organization. The two best examples I have seen is how General Electric uses their intranet, an internal communication device that accomplishes two things for General Electric. First, all successful DMAIC and DMADV projects are posted on their intranet, which allow other General Electric personnel to learn from successful projects. Second, it is used as a clearinghouse for information and identification of projects already completed within General Electric which prevents duplication of efforts.

Lithonia Lighting uses their intranet in a similar fashion. The latest projects are chronicled, project teams are recognized, and various tutorials on subjects are listed.

➤ The Business Quality Council

In *The Six Sigma Revolution,* I discussed how a Business Quality Council should be structured. When your Business Quality Council is up and running, the minutes should be communicated throughout the organization. This accomplishes several key objectives. First and foremost, it provides a status throughout the organization of the strategic elements of Six Sigma. For example, revisions to core or key subprocesses will occur at the Business Quality Council. This change must be communicated quickly because it impacts employees and management alike.

The Council provides information regarding management's ongoing involvement with Six Sigma which has multiple benefits among the workforce. Knowing management is actively involved in Six Sigma is a sign of good leadership. When an executive role-models the behaviors expected of others, it dramatically helps to sustain and grow Six Sigma in an organization. .

■ HOW TO CHANGE JOB STRUCTURES IN YOUR ORGANIZATION STRATEGICALLY

In this final section of Chapter 5, we address how job structures must be changed or modified in order to be successful with Six Sigma. We discuss job structures in two ways. First, the strategic elements that Six Sigma will impact in your job structures, and secondly we talk about the tactical changes that must be addressed.

As we have repeatedly discussed in both this book and *The Six Sigma Revolution,* the most important strategic element of a Six Sigma initiative is the creation and maintenance of the Business Process Management System. The major job structure affected by implementing Business Process Management is the establishment of process owners. While creating process owners should not impact the organizational chart, nonetheless, this is a significant change in managerial responsibility.

Process owners should be those individuals who experience the greatest pain or gain in the process, are considered subject matter experts in that process, have the respect of people in the preceding and subsequent processes, and present a general aptitude toward process improvement. Most executives and management will be process owners at either the core or key subprocess level. It is important to recognize a small minority of nonmanagers will make ideal process owners. While we don't recommend any special compensation, it is important to recognize these process owners on an equal level as executives or managers who are process owners. Any signs of less respect for nonmanagers in the position of a process owner will soon send the message throughout the organization that the traditional functional alignment and its concurrent stature is more important than the process owner. This needs to be carefully managed by the business leader. Perry Monych at GE Access has done this well by insuring that each and every process owner is given the same credibility and time considerations during their report outs in the Business Quality Council. One method he uses quite well is to ensure that no organizational authority would control decision making in a meeting. If I am coaching a Business Quality Council and I can observe informally a difference in the way the traditional business leaders and the newly created nonmanagement process owners are treated in meetings, I know the client is headed for trouble. With Perry's meetings, I knew all would have equal "say."

At the tactical level, job descriptions need to be dramatically changed in most organizations. The major change required is for the Human Resources function to take responsibility for including process improvement in everyone's job description.

In most organizations that hire me to implement Six Sigma I find that most employees, regardless of their position on the organization chart, somehow don't see process improvement as part of their job description. Often I hear the refrain, "I already work 12 hours a day and now I am required to spend time on improvement projects." I have used a variety of analogies and metaphors to change this mindset with only limited results. For example, as mentioned earlier in the book, I ask how long the participants' cars would run if they spent no time servicing the car, getting the oil changed, getting a tune up, and the like. During the time the car is being serviced, the car is not available for travel, yet no one disputes the importance of car maintenance. I have described some organizations as lumberjacks who spend no time in maintenance or sharpening of their tools and expect the same performance with a dull tool as they do with a freshly sharpened tool. I have attempted to take the last example and ask participants to describe psychologically what it's like to work clearing a field of redwoods with a dull ax and then attempt to transfer that discussion to what it's like working in a organization that doesn't set the expectation of process improvement as part of each and every job description.

My attempts at persuading my audience are often unsuccessful. It is better to modify job descriptions to include process improvement as an expectation for everyone in the organization. Further, I encourage organizations to set a tone for this critical element of Six Sigma to be included in all employee orientations so that any individual who comes on board will see that process improvement is a part of the job.

While the typical organization, before implementation of Six Sigma, spends half of its time inefficiently, I also recommend to management that goals and objectives for individuals and business units be modified to take into consideration this job expectation, at least temporarily, knowing the potential cost savings of devoting time to process improvement.

■ SUMMARY

This chapter addressed how management can create and sustain the systems and structures that determine the Six Sigma culture. They include:

➤ Hiring Six Sigma people in your organization.

➤ Developing Six Sigma people in your organization.

➤ Evaluating Six Sigma behaviors in your organization.

➤ Rewarding and recognizing Six Sigma behaviors in your organization.

➤ Communicating Six Sigma in your organization.

➤ Changing job structures in your organization strategically (Business Process Management) and tactically (Six Sigma Job Descriptions, Roles, and Responsibilities).

KEY LEARNINGS

➤ The key positions to initiate and maintain Six Sigma in an organization are the Quality Leader, the Master Black Belt, and Black/Green Belts.

➤ The Quality Leader and the Master Black Belts should be internal hires. The Quality Leader must be politically sensitive, knowing when to push executives, but not be the proverbial "bull in the china shop."

➤ Master Black Belts must be experts in the technical areas of Six Sigma, the strategies of Business Process Management, and Facilitative Leadership.

➤ Development of the organization's employees should include ongoing training of various types. The most common training courses should be the Six Sigma Overview, Business Process Management, Green Belt for Champions Training, Black/Green Belt Training, Change Management, Facilitative Management, and individual tool clinics.

➤ Quality Leader's evaluations should be based on how well they help shape the strategic elements of Six Sigma.

➤ Master Black Belts' and Key Black Belts' evaluations should be based on technical knowledge, training ability,

(Continued)

project results, and requests for assistance from teams and/or management.

➤ Evaluation of individual contributors should be based on participation in project teams when requested, acceptance of the role of process owner and project Champion, if applicable, attendance at all necessary training, implementation of the response plans for other project team's work if they are affected by the plan to either implement solutions or control the process after improvement.

➤ Reward and recognition is an important element in the creation of a Six Sigma culture. Care should be given to insuring fairness and balance between the bonuses for the management group and individual contributors. We recommend gain sharing for individual contributors.

➤ Communication of the Six Sigma initiative is a critical success factor for Six Sigma. There are multiple venues for communication to take place to sustain Six Sigma. They include: the Six Sigma kick-off; communications to the financial community; the all-managers' meetings; managerial updates at staff meetings (particularly having Six Sigma the first thing on the agenda); using Six Sigma as a marketing tool in communications; communicating, and working with suppliers; circulating success stories on your intranet and utilization of the Business Quality Council.

➤ Job structures need to be changed strategically (describing the role of the process owner) and tactically (including process improvement in all job descriptions).

Measuring the Six Sigma Culture

Any reading of Six Sigma literature shows an emphasis on measurement. Process dashboards, critical-to-quality (CTQ) measures, customer satisfaction measures—the list is virtually endless. With such a focus on measures, I have found it peculiar that little discussion has centered on the importance of measuring the Six Sigma climate.

First, let me stress what this chapter is *not*. We will not discuss measures of processes or products or services. We will not focus on the measures traditionally associated with Six Sigma. This should not be considered an abandonment of these measures, only to say that they are located in other texts, including *The Six Sigma Revolution*.

Instead, this chapter will focus on measuring how well Six Sigma has been "baked" into your organization. Specifically, how to mathematically calculate the formula we introduced in Chapter 1, the $Q \times A = E$ formula. I detail what specific elements you should grade yourself on relative to Q and then detail the specific elements associated with A.

I define a passing grade. I then share various client profiles to show you how organizations that have attempted to implement Six Sigma have succeeded (and why), and how some organizations have either produced marginal results or failed altogether.

■ MEASURING THE QUALITY OF YOUR TECHNICAL SIX SIGMA ACTIVITIES

Quality *(Q)* measures are made up of the following:

1. The degree to which the organization has created the Six Sigma business process management system (strategic).

2. The degree to which Six Sigma training is effective and efficient.

3. The degree to which your Six Sigma consulting has been effective and efficient.

4. The effectiveness of your Six Sigma project management.

5. The effectiveness of your Six Sigma infrastructure (Quality Leadership, Master Black Belts, Black and Green Belts).

I briefly describe each of these elements after I present the grid for scoring them.

When an organization is ready to evaluate their progress on both Q and A, I present to them the grids in Figures 6.1 and 6.2. Along the horizontal axis are the five Q measures mentioned above. Along the vertical axis is a Likert Scale ranging from zero (a low rating for the item in question) to five (the highest rating for the item in question). (Figure 6.2 is the grid we will use later in this chapter for A.) Now let's examine the explanations for the Q elements to see how an organization should rate themselves against each of the criteria.

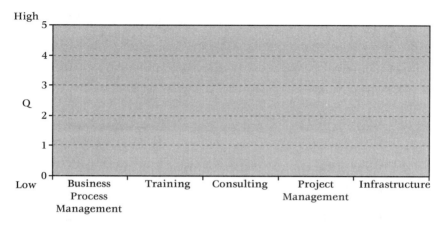

Figure 6.1   Quality of Your Technical Six Sigma Activities

➤ The Degree to Which the Organization Has Created the Six Sigma Business Process Management System (Strategic)

This first and most important Q element refers to how well the executive team has created and sustained the business

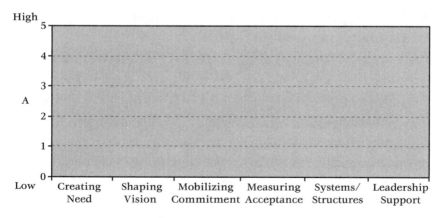

Figure 6.2   Acceptance

process management element of Six Sigma. Specifically, the rating incorporates how well the organization has:

➤ Identified and communicated the strategic business objectives of the organization.

➤ Identified the core, key sub, and enabling processes of the organization.

➤ Identified the process owners at the core, key sub, and enabling process level.

➤ Identified the measures that constitute the key measures of effectiveness and efficiency for each process (the process dashboard).

➤ Data collection has occurred and is ongoing for all relevant processes.

➤ Determined project selection criteria.

➤ Formally applied project selection criteria in selecting DMAIC or DMADV projects.

➤ Managed projects and processes on an ongoing basis.

➤ The Degree to Which Your Six Sigma Training Is Effective and Efficient

In Chapter 5, I discussed the various courses that constitute a successful Six Sigma curriculum. Also discussed in Chapter 5 was the methodology on how to teach the courses. Yet, no matter how detailed our discussion, in the wrong hands the class can result in confusion and frustration on the part of the participants. As part of your rating of Q, evaluation of the effectiveness and efficiency of the training should be completed.

A guide to how effective and efficient the training is should be based primarily on a review of course evaluations (after all, this is a type of customer survey). A good course evaluation should include:

➤ Practical value of the course.

➤ New ideas generated.

➤ Relevance of the training to project.

➤ Pace of training.

➤ Instructor knowledge of subject.

➤ Instructor ability to deliver.

➤ The Degree to Which Your Six Sigma Consulting Has Been Effective and Efficient

It is virtually impossible to implement Six Sigma without some external help in the first year or so of implementation. In Chapter 5, we discussed hiring a Six Sigma consultant. If your Six Sigma consultant did training, some of the questions listed in the previous section can be used in part to evaluate the effectiveness and efficiency of your Six Sigma consultant.

However, training effectiveness is only one part of what a good consultant should be evaluated on. While course evaluations are a part of the examination of a good consultant, I recommend the Quality Leader obtain feedback from business leaders (to obtain information on how well the consultant facilitated the business process management elements of Six Sigma implementation) and the Master Black Belts and Key Black Belts (to determine how well the consultant did on project consulting and "train the trainer" consulting, if applicable).

➤ The Effectiveness of Your Six Sigma Project Management

Once DMAIC or DMADV projects are selected, project management plays a large role in the success of projects. As mentioned in Chapter 5, a core competency of the Black or Green Belt is her or his ability to guide the team throughout the "tollgates" of the DMAIC or DMADV methodology. In addition to the Black Belt or Green Belt, evaluation of project management should also include how well the project Champion conducts his or her role.

➤ The Effectiveness of Your Six Sigma Infrastructure (Quality Leadership, Master Black Belts, Black and Green Belts)

We discussed the core competencies of each of the critical positions within an organization's Six Sigma infrastructure. Having these positions is one thing. Filling them with competent, achievement-oriented people is another thing altogether. The evaluation of effectiveness and efficiency of how well they have accomplished their tasks should be done by the executive staff and preferably your external consultant.

The recommendation to have an external consultant be part of this evaluation is based on the fact that executives may place too much responsibility for the success or lack thereof on their quality personnel.

■ MEASURING THE ACCEPTANCE OF YOUR SIX SIGMA ACTIVITIES

In the preceding pages, we reviewed briefly the elements that should be evaluated for the Q of the $Q \times A = E$ formula. Here are the elements that need to be evaluated for the A measures.

1. Creating the need for Six Sigma.

2. Shaping the Six Sigma Vision.

3. Mobilizing commitment to Six Sigma and managing resistance.

4. Measuring acceptance of the Six Sigma culture.

5. Modifying the systems and structures affecting Six Sigma.

6. Six Sigma leadership.

We already addressed in detail each of the these elements. In previous chapters, we described how an organization should create the need for Six Sigma, shape a vision, mobilize commitment, and modify the systems and structures that affect Six Sigma. The activities we describe next constitute measuring the acceptance of the Six Sigma culture. Chapter 7 addresses Six Sigma leadership, which you will see is not the same thing as evaluating your Six Sigma infrastructure.

➤ Measuring the Six Sigma Culture

I encourage an executive team to do this exercise approximately nine months into their implementation effort. Usually I recommend this exercise be placed on the Business

Quality Council agenda shortly after completion of the Business Process Management creation and the completion of the first wave of projects so that at least a few projects have had a chance for their solutions to be implemented.

At the beginning of the Six Sigma culture measurement session, I quickly review each of the elements in both the Q and A profiles and clarify any questions before the rating begins. Typically, the audience present is the organization's executive team and the process owners who constitute the Business Quality Council.

We then begin what is called a "fist-to-five" exercise. Here I take each of the elements in the Q and A profiles and ask each executive present to stick up a fist (meaning the organization has done nothing in that area) to a hand raised with up to five fingers showing (five fingers indicating that the organization was excelling in that area).

There may be upwards of 15 to 20 executives present for this exercise. I tell each of these participants that if there is a range of less than 3 for any given element for either profile, I will simply add the numbers seen and calculate an average. If there is a range of 3 or more, then I will request the high and low raters to briefly discuss the rationale behind their vote. Once this brief discussion has taken place, another vote is taken and regardless of the range, the overall average is calculated. Below are two examples:

Example 1

Rate how well you have created your Business Process Management System.

Answers of 14 participants:

4, 3, 5, 4, 3, 5, 4, 4, 4, 5, 3, 3, 4, 5

*With the range less than 3, we simply add up the 14 re-
spondent numbers and divide by 14. We get 56 divided
by 14 or 4.0.*

Example 2

*Rate how well you have practiced effective and efficient
project management relative to the first-wave projects.*

Answer of 14 participants:

3, 3, 5, 2, 4, 3, 5, 2, 3, 5, 2, 4, 5, 2

*Here we have a range of 3 (with the highest vote regis-
tering a 5 and the lowest vote garnering a 2). In this
case, I request a brief discussion explaining why the 5s
and 2s voted the way they did.*

*For this question, the clarifying discussion proved
worthwhile. The 5s indicated their vote was based on
the perception that all of the first-wave projects were
managed as successfully as the projects they were personally involved in while the 2s felt everyone's projects
were as bad as theirs. Then we heard from some of the
3s and 4s who described their vote as what they perceived the overall project management of all first-wave
projects. With the issue clarified, I asked for a revote
that looked as follows:*

3, 3, 3, 4, 3, 3, 2, 4, 4, 3, 4, 4, 3, 4

*Here we now generate a more representative 3.36 for the
average.*

Completing this exercise is done by getting an average
rating for each of the elements for both the Q and A profiles.
Once these profiles are completed, I multiply each Q and A
average by two and get an overall average. Why not just use a

1 to 10 scale to begin with? The Likert Scale is named after a University of Michigan statistician who mathematically proved that a 1–5 or 1–7 scale is more mathematically accurate than a 1–10 scale. Likert found that when a 1–10 scale is used, people rarely use the middle numbers (3, 4, 5, 6) and either vote low (1 or 2) or high (7, 8, 9, 10). Thus, the use of a 1–5 scale which we later multiply × 2.

In the example that follows, we see averages for both the Q and A profiles for a recent client:

Q	Rating
Business Process Management System	$3.8 \times 2 = 7.6$
Six Sigma training	$4.4 \times 2 = 8.8$
Six Sigma consulting	$4.2 \times 2 = 8.4$
Project management	$3.1 \times 2 = 6.2$
Six Sigma infrastructure	$4.6 \times 2 = 9.2$
Overall average	8.04

A	Rating
Creating the need for Six Sigma	$3.1 \times 2 = 6.2$
Shaping the Six Sigma Vision	$1.3 \times 2 = 2.6$
Mobilizing commitment to Six Sigma and managing resistance	$1.1 \times 2 = 2.2$
Modifying the systems and structures affecting Six Sigma	$1.5 \times 2 = 3.0$
Measuring the acceptance of the Six Sigma culture	$0.0 \times 2 = 0.0$
Six Sigma leadership	$2.2 \times 2 = 4.4$
Overall average	3.07

As we indicated in Chapter 1, the $Q \times A = E$ formula is multiplicative. We would now multiply 8.04 (Q) by 3.06 (A) to arrive at an overall Six Sigma Culture rating of 24.6.

What does a 24.7 rating mean? Approximately 30 percent of my clients have achieved a cultural transformation, about 50 percent have achieved a tactical return on investment, and about 20 percent have totally wasted the money they invested in their Six Sigma effort. Here is the general $Q \times A = E$ numbers associated with these categories:

$Q \times A = E$ Score	Results
0–20	Wasted their money on Six Sigma.
21–40	Some tactical results, initiative will likely die.
41–60	Significant tactical results, initiative will focus on projects for the life of Six Sigma.
61–80	Cultural transformation, but may take some time.
81–100	Cultural transformation, a world-class Six Sigma organization.

Therefore, this example is an organization that has generated tactical results. However, failure to take corrective action (especially on the A of the $Q \times A$ formula) will result in this organization probably generating another wave of Black or Green Belt training and, irrespective of the results, the initiative will die with a whimper.

The executives who commit to a Six Sigma initiative need to periodically take the pulse of how well their initiative is going; not just in terms of increased profitability, increased productivity, or cost savings due to projects. As you can see, all of the above ratings show some results except the first category. Failure to measure the Six Sigma culture may lull executives into thinking they are on course to be a Six Sigma success story when they may be nurturing the seeds of ultimate failure.

We next review various client profiles of both successful and unsuccessful initiatives, focusing on where the client was and what the client needed to do to take corrective action in order to improve their chances to become a world-class Six Sigma culture.

All of the subsequent case studies are true. Due to the proprietary nature of the data, no specific client names are used.

■ CASE STUDY 1—SIX SIGMA CULTURE MEASURE

Our first case study is a Six Sigma client who became interested in embracing Six Sigma after they heard about General Electric's efforts. Their executive team was genuinely interested in the productivity gains generated by General Electric and was initially committed to doing what was right with regard to Six Sigma. Nearly a year into their effort, they were dissatisfied. I recommended the executive team conduct a Six Sigma cultural measure (the results are shown in Figures 6.3 and 6.4).

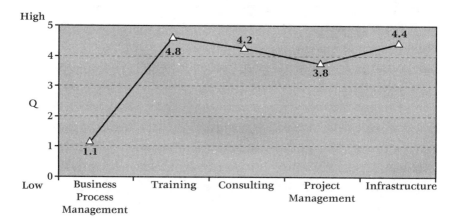

Figure 6.3 Case Study 1—Quality of Your Technical Six Sigma Activities

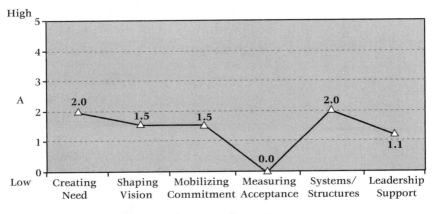

Figure 6.4 Case Study 1—Acceptance

The $Q \times A = E$ formula works out to $7.3 \times 2.7 = 19.71$. The overall analysis shows this client well on the way to being a Six Sigma failure, an organization that has totally wasted their Six Sigma investment. Of course I didn't begin with telling them they were on their way to being one of my unmitigated failures. What I did in this consulting day was first focus on their strengths (which you will shortly see are significant) and then look at their deltas (areas they need to change) and what corrective action would be necessary for them to change their chances to becoming a world-class Six Sigma organization.

➤ Case Study 1—Pluses

Six Sigma Training. Eckes and Associates, Inc. provided the first wave of training and it was very well received. Black Belts warmly embraced the opportunity to improve existing processes that were broken. One of the projects was a DMADV project to create a new business acquisition process that went on to be a major success.

Six Sigma Infrastructure. The client had tapped one of their manufacturing vice presidents to be the Quality Leader and this individual had performed well in most areas save one. Their Master Black Belts were competent in all areas of the technical elements of Six Sigma and had done well coaching the first wave of projects.

Project Management Skills. While there was some drop off of the rating of this element, project management was still considered a strength of this client's Six Sigma work. It is important to note stratification of the data, however. The first wave of training was rated in the high 4s while the second wave hovered around 3. The reason for this is discussed with the deltas.

Six Sigma Consulting. Any rating above 3 usually warrants the element being rated a plus. Some of my associates provided on-site consulting to assist the first wave of projects to achieve success.

➤ Case Study 1 – Deltas

Business Process Management. Six Sigma is more than projects. When an organization sees Six Sigma as nothing more than tactical projects, there is no way the organization will achieve a cultural transformation. As we have repeatedly advocated, Six Sigma is first and foremost a management philosophy. We will see through these case studies that most failures to achieve cultural transformation is a result of failing to manage the A of the $Q \times A$ formula. It is also common that a failure to achieve better results is a direct result of poorly managing the business process management element of the Q part of the profile. It was this area that was the one area that the Quality Leader had not spent sufficient time with his peers.

Measuring Acceptance of the Six Sigma Culture. The first time we conduct measurement of the culture this will usually be rated around a zero. The important test is if this measurement remains a zero in future evaluations. In the case of this client, it was the one and only time a formal measure was conducted.

Six Sigma Leadership. As we will see discussed in Chapter 7, leaders must lead the effort with more than allocation of funds for consultants or training. As evident by the failure of this client to sustain their business process management activities, Six Sigma leadership had to be rated a delta. [*Author's note:* Initially the executive team rated themselves higher than the 1.1 registered in the profile above. It was my input that made this executive team reevaluate their rating.]

Virtually All Other A Elements. Despite my discussions in the first days consulting with this client regarding the importance of the executive team addressing the A of Six Sigma, management ignored my input on this critical element. From creating the need for Six Sigma, to shaping the vision and dealing with the resistance (which for this client became more prominent after the first wave of projects), the A of this client's Six Sigma initiative was largely ignored.

➤ Case Study 1 – Corrective Action Recommendations

The beauty of doing this cultural assessment is that corrective action nicely follows. I recommended their first priority was to readdress their commitment to Business Process Management. During the close of this Business Quality Council meeting, we made agreements for the executive team to address the following items in the next three months. The Quality Leader requested my return at that time to review and comment on progress on:

➤ Reevaluation of the core key sub and enabling processes.

➤ Modification of the Process Owners.

➤ Recommitment to key subprocess dashboard measures.

➤ Reconfiguration of project selection criteria.

In addition to these steps on the one area of Q that was still a weakness, the other major modifications were in the A of their quality effort:

➤ Spend a Business Quality Council meeting creating a short-/long-term threat/opportunity matrix that would standardize the need for this client's Six Sigma effort. From this exercise, have each process owner communicate these threats and opportunities during process staff meetings.

➤ At the same time, the Business Quality Council creates and communicates the vision, results, and behaviors of their Six Sigma culture. This was also suggested to be communicated at the process staff meetings.

➤ At a subsequent Business Quality Council meeting it was suggested the Council address their systems and structures as referenced in Chapter 5, for them, most notably in the area of reward and communication.

➤ Case Study 1 – Update

I was brought back three times over the next nine months to facilitate Business Quality Council meetings. These meetings were productive and at the last meeting, the $Q \times A$ formula had risen from 19.71 to the mid-40s. They would no longer be one of my 20 percent failures. Their problem, however, was that more work was done during the meetings I facilitated then when I wasn't there. At this writing, I have no plans to return to this client and I would anticipate them being rated one of the 50 percent of clients that derive tactical results for the duration of their efforts.

■ CASE STUDY 2—SIX SIGMA CULTURE MEASURE

This client was an acquisition of General Electric in the late 1990s. A highly successful company in their own right, after being acquired by General Electric they were mandated to implement Six Sigma. Due to the sensitivity of being acquired, General Electric asked me to be the lead consultant to start their Six Sigma effort. During our first phone contact, I was told by their quality leader that there would be no need to spend any time on Business Process Management as they had already had a quality program prior to being purchased by General Electric and that my work in that area would be redundant. It was at this point I made the mistake of acquiescing to this claim, rather than checking it out for myself.

In conjunction with not doing the Business Process Management effort, I was told that projects had already been selected based on their quality program that was in place prior to being acquired by General Electric. In defense of my decision, I believe that any organization that has had a quality initiative prior to implementing Six Sigma needs to have Six Sigma be built on what has come before it. I congratulate an organization for first attempting a prior quality effort. I then further congratulate and try to build Six Sigma into their previous efforts. Nonetheless, I should have done more homework on this client, and more importantly insisted on going through the Business Process Management consulting.

The project training was difficult yet productive. Instead of Black Belt training, project training was directed toward all project team members. Resistance was rampant through all sessions. This client was resistant to being a new General Electric business. I vividly remember the tent cards for people to write their names in front of everyone's desk being those that I had sent from Connecticut having the General Electric logo. Ten minutes to go before the first class started, their training director went around picking up the General Electric tent cards and replacing them with tent cards of the acquired company.

During the class, questions asked of me were of the type that manifested resistance of a strong cultural type (see Chapter 3). Among the questions that bombarded me each and every time I visited them were:

➤ "There isn't anything new in Six Sigma, is there? It seems just a more complicated methodology that we have here anyway."

➤ "Don't you have any examples that directly apply to our type of insurance business? I mean, all of your insurance examples are from General Electric."

➤ "Isn't this approach just a way for General Electric to show its control over us?"

Questions of this type tried my patience, but I attempted to put myself in their shoes and be empathic. The truth of the matter was that there was overlap between the Six Sigma initiative and the initiative they had previously, but their initiative wasn't producing the results that General Electric was getting with Six Sigma. Midway through the first wave of training I was concerned with their projects, but as the saying goes, "the most meaningless statistic in sports is the halftime score."

Despite the training being difficult, the first wave of projects produced significant results. Having met my requirements to jump-start their Six Sigma initiative, I thought I had completed my assignment with this client, only to be called six months later by General Electric to visit this client to attend and comment on a Business Quality Council meeting.

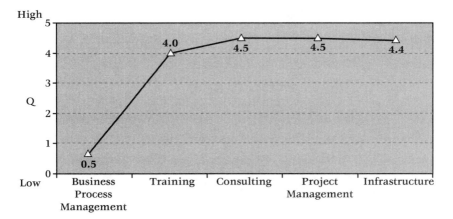

Figure 6.5 Case Study 2—Quality of your Technical Six Sigma Activities

Despite some grousing about Six Sigma, I pulled out my trusty Six Sigma culture measure profiles and we completed Figures 6.5 (on page 165) and 6.6.

Their score of 33.87 showed what they already knew. They had achieved solid tactical results in their first wave of training. But a score of 33.87 showed that continuation of their current level of support would result in their initiative dying a slow and painful death. This death would be particularly painful as they were now a General Electric business unit. I quickly reviewed with them their pluses and deltas, knowing corrective action would be necessary for them to be a true General Electric Six Sigma success story.

➤ Case Study 2 — Pluses

Six Sigma Training. Despite the pain to me, the consultant, overall they felt training had been a strength of their first wave of projects.

Six Sigma Consulting. General Electric Master Black Belts had provided consulting and the host General Electric

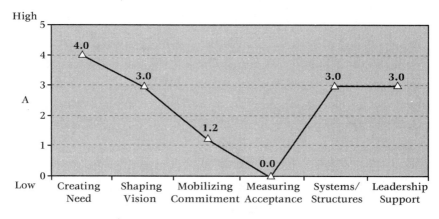

Figure 6.6 Case Study 2 — Acceptance

business had among them the best Six Sigma Master Black Belts I had ever worked with.

Project Management Skills. This client's previous quality effort had already shown the importance of project management skills. Their efforts here were without question.

Six Sigma Infrastructure. Again, their previous quality effort had resulted in the creation of a talented and proactive group of quality leaders and specialists.

Creating the Need for Six Sigma. While I initially questioned the high number this client gave to the A of Six Sigma, they actually had committed to creating the need for Six Sigma through a threat/opportunity matrix that had focused on the merger with General Electric.

Shaping a Vision. While less impressive than the work created in showing the need for Six Sigma, I was impressed with the work of the previous quality effort around the vision, results, and behaviors of their previous quality initiative that applied to Six Sigma.

Systems and Structures. While not world-class, their previous quality effort had manifested changes in their reward and recognition program as well as how they hired and developed their staff.

➤ Case Study 2—Deltas

Business Process Management. Clearly my mistake in not addressing this item was pivotal in their overall low score. Their previous quality effort was a tactical quality effort, albeit successful. Here I was guilty of allowing their previous effort to forgo the major way Six Sigma was different than previous quality efforts, a strategic management effort rather than just another approach to gain productivity without a change in the way executives manage the business.

Mobilizing Commitment. While registering some activity, by far the major reason this client wasn't further along in their Six Sigma effort was due to not managing the resistance of having to do Six Sigma as a result of a merger with General Electric. Specifically, there was massive and widespread organizational resistance to being acquired by General Electric. Thus, a manifestation of this resistance was aimed at the Six Sigma initiative required to be a General Electric acquisition. This became the focus of our Six Sigma corrective action.

➤ Case Study 2 — Corrective Action Recommendations

The focus of this client's corrective action was two-fold. I strongly recommended the executive team redirect their efforts toward creation of the Business Process Management System. The second major corrective action was to develop a more formalized strategy to overcome the entrenched cultural resistance this organization had toward their acquisition by General Electric. This included strengthening their planning for influence strategies, utilizing a company wide threat/opportunity matrix and a company-wide vision of what Six Sigma can do for the organization. You might also remember that a key strategy for dealing with organizational resistance is a modification of the Six Sigma implementation effort so that there is greater ownership on the part of the organization.

➤ **Case Study 2—Update**

To the credit of this organization, they agreed to and participated in a two day session for Business Process Management. These days went moderately well as we created the core, key sub, and enabling processes of this insurance business. In some cases, the work was confirmatory of their previous efforts. The major focus of the two days was trying to create the process dashboard measures. We tentatively identified those measures. For those of you familiar with process dashboard creation, you know that what is brainstormed in the classroom must be validated during the intersession. Knowing this to be the next step in the process of creating the Business Process Management System, I told them to call me when they were ready to proceed with the next steps in the process. I never received a call. Needless to say, I am also unaware of how well they readdressed the cultural resistance to Six Sigma. Put this one in the failure column.

■ CASE STUDY 3—SIX SIGMA CULTURE MEASURE

The two preceding examples of less than sterling results were in large part a result of poor Business Process Management Systems and a general failure to address the A in the $Q \times A$ formula.

In this example, we review a rare but occasionally occurring reason for not being further along in a Six Sigma initiative. That is, problems with the Q of the $Q \times A$ formula. Figures 6.7 and 6.8 show the company profile.

This client's combined score, multiplying $Q \times A$, is 20.32. A review of their profile shows lower scores for Q than A (though A is substandard as well). A review of their pluses:

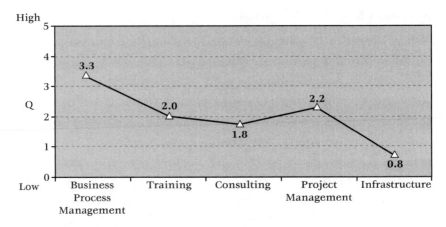

Figure 6.7 Case Study 3—Quality of Your Technical
Six Sigma Activities

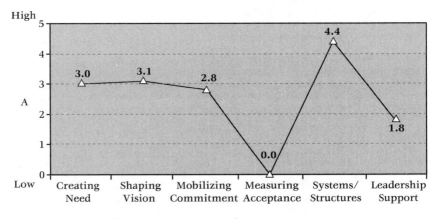

Figure 6.8 Case Study 3—Acceptance

➤ Case Study 3 – Pluses

Systems and Structures. This client had a strong Human Resource Director. As a result, they had done well incorporating Six Sigma skills into their interviewing and hiring process. In addition, the Human Resource Director developed an orientation program incorporating Six Sigma as well as developing a vibrant reward and recognition program.

Business Process Management System. The client had hired me to assist them create their Business Process Management System. This system was created well and would have been rated even higher if they had placed more emphasis on managing it's use rather than just participation in its creation.

➤ Case Study 3 – Deltas

The Six Sigma Infrastructure. The biggest mistake this company had made was in the hiring of their quality leader and support staff. Despite my urging you to hire your "best and brightest," they had selected their traditional quality leader who had a traditional inspection background who, in turn, had hired inspection managers as Master Black Belts. This selection turned out to be a disaster on several levels. This individual not only did not develop the skills in Six Sigma, he actually had resistance to Six Sigma. His Master Black Belts were no better. Collectively, they did not maintain the Business Process Management System we originally created prior to the first series of projects.

Six Sigma Training and Consulting. This client wished not to have my staff assist in training or consulting for the first projects. They chose to use a computer-based training program. While there is nothing wrong with this approach overall, I had recommended that their first wave of training be done with a person teaching. I indicated to them that one of the goals of the first wave of training is not just to educate the audience on the tools and techniques but to create enthusiasm among the Black Belts for the first wave of training, so that these Black Belts become your evangelists for future employees in your organization. As a result, commitment on the part of the Black Belts was passive at best (perhaps a subconscious goal of the Quality Leader).

While there were other significant deltas which included areas around acceptance of Six Sigma within the organization, their biggest issue was their Six Sigma infrastructure.

➤ Case Study 3 — Corrective Action Recommendations

One of the advantages of being an established consultant is that you can "call 'em like you seem 'em." I informed this client that they had made a mistake in their choice of their Quality Leader and his support staff and that, without a major overhaul of their quality infrastructure, they were headed for failure in their Six Sigma effort.

➤ Case Study 3 — Update

When I work with a client to expedite their Six Sigma progress, I always think of Confucius' words, "The thousand mile journey begins with the first step." Without a change in this client's Six Sigma infrastructure, all other modifications would have been halfheartedly implemented. Despite my encouragement to make a change in the infrastructure, this client was committed to making their Six Sigma initiative work with the incumbent Quality Leader. Today, I really don't know if this client is a Six Sigma success or not. Another benefit of being an established Six Sigma consultant is being able to fire a client. Sadly, this is what happened.

■ CASE STUDY 4—SIX SIGMA CULTURE MEASURE

At this point, you are probably tired of hearing about those clients that either have failed outright or are only going to get tactical results for the duration of their effort. In our last two case studies, I am going to share with you two stories of clients I believe are examples of Six Sigma cultural transformation success stories. It is no coincidence that both are General Electric examples.

The first of these cultural transformations is GE Capital Commercial Equipment Finance (CEF). I began work with GE Capital CEF in the late 1990s. GE Capital had developed the Green Belt for Champions course that I have referenced in Chapter 5 of this book. Bill Lindenfelder and I provided the first wave of training, working with their management. At that time, GE Capital CEF had just won the President's Award at General Electric, indicative of an organization that personified not only the results desired of a General Electric business but the values as well. When we began working with CEF, they clearly were not only meeting the requirements of being a General Electric business but exceeding them as well. During our first training session, both Bill and I were met with polite but direct questions about Six Sigma.

This was an organization that frankly was succeeding in their goals and objectives without Six Sigma. However, they were blessed with perhaps one of the best Six Sigma infrastructures I had ever been a part of. Michele Landis, their Quality Leader, was strongly committed to Six Sigma and had built both a terrific Six Sigma infrastructure and had worked with their management to create one of the best Business Process Management Systems in the GE Capital businesses I had seen. When Bill Lindenfelder and I began training their executives, we were quickly aware that this was a business that was capable of using Six Sigma to take them to the next level.

During the Green Belt for Champions' training of their management, Chris Richmond, their business leader, showed both support and legitimate skepticism about Six Sigma. He embraced much of the Six Sigma methodology, not only at the tactical level but supported the Business Process Management elements as well. Chris Richmond ended up being one of the General Electric business leaders I respected the most. I didn't spend much personal time with Chris, but he was a business leader who supported what he saw as an aid in helping him support his business goals and questioned what he thought was the bureaucracy of Six Sigma. During the time I worked with CEF, he ended up purchasing a business called Simuflite, a company that trains pilots through the use of aircraft simulators. Long will I remember Chris giving the opening remarks for Six Sigma training for the Simuflite executive training. As he kicked off the training I was to do for Simuflite, without reference to any notes, he genuinely talked about several CEF Six Sigma success stories, the need to manage by process rather than function and the importance of seeing Six Sigma as a management philosophy rather than a cost-savings tactical initiative. The speech to Simuflite was among the best that I have heard. What particularly impressed me was that there was no "fluff" in the speech. While Chris talked from the

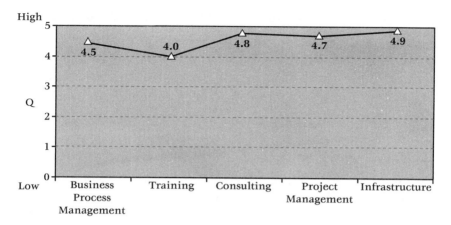

Figure 6.9 Case Study 4—Quality of Your Technical Six Sigma Activities

heart, he was honest and candid about Six Sigma. Thus, I was not surprised when after one year into their Six Sigma initiative Michele Landis, their Quality Leader at the time, produced the data that generated Figures 6.9 and 6.10.

CEF's $Q \times A$ equals 72.09. This was an amazing first cultural measurement number. Virtually all of their Six Sigma

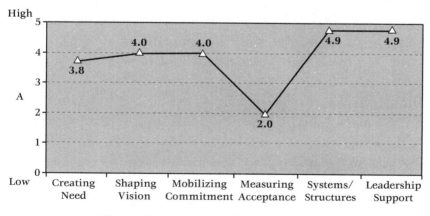

Figure 6.10 Case Study 4—Acceptance

activities were considered a strength. Continued commitment to their initiative and sustaining their effort was simply a matter of continuing their current performance. CEF is an example of this being the case. Michele Landis went on to assist the CEF e-commerce effort. At first, I thought this would detract from their Six Sigma effort. My concerns were ill founded. With the likes of Rob Phillips, a proactive Master Black Belt who understood both the tactical and strategic elements of Six Sigma, CEF remains a true Six Sigma cultural success story for General Electric.

■ CASE STUDY 5—SIX SIGMA CULTURE MEASURE

Our last Six Sigma culture measure is yet another General Electric success story. The client is General Electric Access, an acquisition of General Electric in the late 1990s. Located in Boulder, Colorado, my first attraction to this client was working with someone located less than 10 minutes from my home. No matter how successful you are as a consultant, getting on a plane and traveling somewhere on a Sunday or Monday is not a joyous occasion. Therefore, in 1998, when Perry Monych called me to assist in their Six Sigma effort, I was first and foremost thrilled with an opportunity to work with a local client and then a client that was General Electric.

I was a bit leery in taking this assignment. General Electric Access was previously known in Boulder as Access Graphics, the software company founded by John Ramsey that had made a big impact in the Boulder area in the mid-1990s and an even bigger impact on the national scene a few years later in 1996 when his daughter, JonBenet, was murdered.

I needn't have been leery. General Electric Access, under Perry Monych's leadership, proved to be one of the more impressive businesses I had the pleasure to work with. Perry Monych had taken over for John Ramsey in 1997 after Lockheed (who had previously purchased Access) sold Access Graphics to General Electric. Perry Monych had been a business leader for GE IT Distribution and had been tapped to take on the sensitive post of Business Leader of GE Access.

Six Sigma at GE Access was not an immediate success. They committed in the fall of 1998 to begin with Business Process Management. These sessions to create the process management system were among the best I had been a part of in 20 years of consulting. I did their first wave of Black Belt training and there were sporadic successes.

By the summer of 1999, GE Access had not been the success I thought they could be. Perry Monych and I sat down one day and informally conducted the $Q \times A$ profile. While no numbers were generated, it would have looked like Figures 6.11 and 6.12.

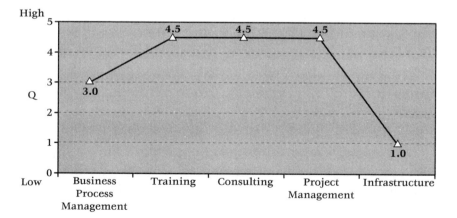

Figure 6.11 Case Study 5—Quality of Your Technical Activities

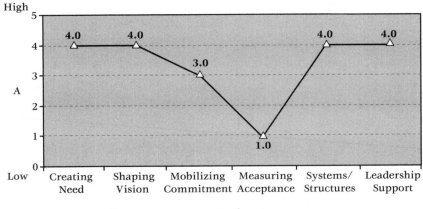

Figure 6.12 Case Study—Acceptance

➤ Case Study 5—Pluses

Business Process Management Creation. As mentioned previously, GE Access had created a superb process management system.

Six Sigma Training. I had provided two waves of training in the first nine months of training that was well received.

Six Sigma Consulting and Project Management Skills. GE Access' management group had done a great job in their Green Belt for Champions course. As a result, they had a committed and knowledgeable group of Champions that resulted in good projects, albeit with sporadic first-wave results.

Creating the Need and Shaping the Vision for Six Sigma. Perry and his direct reports had gone through specific training on change management and had done well in the creation of the need for Six Sigma and shaping the vision of what a Six Sigma company would be at GE Access.

Systems and Structures. Dennis Stoltenberg of GE Access is one of the best Human Resource Directors I have encountered. He combines the competencies in managing the tactical day-to-day items required of a Human Resource Director with a long-term strategic thought process. He had established good interview and hiring practices that incorporated Six Sigma thinking as well as development of a system of rewards and recognition that embodied good Six Sigma thinking.

Six Sigma Leadership. There have been few organizations that have had such strong management. One of the many managerial strengths Perry Monych has is bringing out the leadership skills in others. During an October 1999 strategic planning session, Perry kicked off the meeting and his managers really ran the show. Whether it was John Paget, Michael Minard, or James Walker, each member of the leadership team was a forceful individual within their own right. When it came to Six Sigma commitment, skepticism was mild but what there was of it was directly expressed, which allowed it to be dealt with directly. A Stakeholder Analysis today would show GE Access' management team to be all supportive of Six Sigma, whether moderately or strongly.

➤ Case Study 5 – Deltas

GE Access' deficiencies in their Six Sigma effort were among the more unique I have ever encountered.

Q *Issues.* The biggest Q issue was that prior to Perry coming into the Business Leader position, a GE Access' Quality Leader had been already selected. While a talented individual with a long history of management success, the quality position was a mistaken appointment. This individual's vision for quality at GE Access was tactically focused. While well-intentioned, he was more focused on the minutiae of project work rather than seeing the importance of his strategic responsibilities. After a fruitful beginning at creating their Business Process Management System, this Quality Leader gave only benign support to what we created in October 1998, and instead focused more time on project detail and the creation of his support staff, which led us to the most unique situation I have ever encountered as part of implementing Six Sigma.

Mobilizing Commitment. The staff that GE Access' Quality Leader built were highly intelligent and hard-working Master Black Belts. The problem with this group of Master Black Belts was that they were soon "running the asylum." They had taken the Business Process Management System we had created the previous year and modified it significantly. I pride myself on my flexibility, but all hell broke loose in a Spring 2000 Business Quality Council meeting. With Perry Monych absent, the Master Black Belts proceeded to show process dashboards that were functional measures and projects that had been selected, not by process owners but the Master Black Belts themselves. In all my years of consulting I don't remember such a "spirited" discussion with those that typically are aligned with my efforts philosophically. Upon his return to work, I informed Perry that he had the unique challenge of dealing with mobilizing commitment among his quality infrastructure.

➤ Case Study 5 — Recommendations for Corrective Action/Update

One of the first corrective actions Perry took was to replace the Quality Leader. While painful to this long-standing GE

Access employee, he quickly landed on his feet, taking a high-level operating position with another Colorado company.

The second corrective action was more difficult. Commitment needed to be mobilized among the remaining quality professionals so they were leaders of Six Sigma. At this point, the Master Black Belts were a renegade group of "doers," not facilitators.

I told Perry that the hiring of his new Quality Leader would be among the most important hires of his time at GE Access. Perry initially tried to talk me into taking the position. While many companies had talked to me about taking their quality position, this was the first time in years I actually gave it some thought. Two elements of working for GE Access appealed to me. First and foremost, Perry Monych was clearly the most dynamic, process-oriented leader I had worked with in years. He truly was committed to Six Sigma and saw it as the way to manage his business. Second, taking the GE Access job would mean taking a job for a progressive, highly profitable organization less than 10 miles from home.

While our discussions were serious, they didn't proceed very far. I was aware that I would have to take a pay cut, but once I looked at some preliminary numbers, I realized that there would be no way we could be even close financially.

Once the decision was made that his new Quality Leader was not going to be me, I recommended that he go *outside* his organization for his pick. The new Quality Leader would have to be an outstanding manager, someone with a background of accomplishment and the ability to bring the Master Black Belts under control.

His choice was Janet Burki, an accomplished manager from GE Railcar, a GE Capital company that had a solid reputation for their Six Sigma effort. Perry asked for my opinion on Janet Burki and a lunch was arranged. Less than half an hour into our lunch meeting we were finishing each other's sentences. She was in tune with Business Process Management, a true strategic thinker which was what exactly what GE Access needed in their quality position. In addition, she possessed the management skills needed to redirect, but not demotivate the intelligent Master Black Belts. She guided them into the next wave of Six Sigma projects that turned out far more successful than the first wave of projects.

Today, their $Q \times A = E$ profile would show a significantly high number.

■ SUMMARY

When we associate the word measurement with Six Sigma, we typically think of process dashboards or sigma calculations. This chapter addresses a different type of measurement, that of measurement of your Six Sigma culture.

We revisited the $Q \times A = E$ equation and gave specifics for how to measure both the Q and the A. For Q, we provided the five specifics to measure, namely:

1. The degree to which the organization has created the Six Sigma Business Process Management System (strategic).

2. The degree to which Six Sigma training is effective and efficient.

3. The degree to which Six Sigma consulting has been effective and efficient.

4. The effectiveness of Six Sigma project management.

5. The effectiveness of the Six Sigma infrastructure (Quality Leadership, Master Black Belts, Black and Green Belts).

For *A* we indicated the six areas of Six Sigma acceptance measures, namely:

1. Creating the need for Six Sigma.

2. Shaping the Six Sigma Vision.

3. Mobilizing commitment to Six Sigma and managing resistance.

4. Modifying the systems and structures affecting Six Sigma.

5. Measuring the acceptance of the Six Sigma culture.

6. Six Sigma leadership.

We finished Chapter 6 with five case studies of how the Six Sigma culture was measured and how corrective action was attempted in each case to make the Six Sigma initiative last for each of them.

KEY LEARNINGS

➤ Measurement of the culture of Six Sigma is as important, if not more important, as measurement of processes.

➤ In order for measurement of your Six Sigma culture to be worthwhile, measures must be taken for the technical and strategic elements and the acceptance measures for Six Sigma.

➤ Measures for the Six Sigma culture should be compared to the formula on page 157 to determine the probability of your organization as a Six Sigma success.

(continued)

(Continued)

➤ A Six Sigma culture score of 0 to 20 indicates an organization is wasting their investment on Six Sigma.

➤ A Six Sigma culture score of 21 to 40 indicates the organization is showing tactical results but the initiative likely will die without major corrective action.

➤ A Six Sigma culture score of 41 to 60 indicates the organization has generated tactical results but without corrective action focus on projects will probably be the legacy of the organization relative to Six Sigma.

➤ A Six Sigma culture score of 61 to 80 indicates the organization is on the path toward having a cultural transformation but it may take time.

➤ A Six Sigma culture score of 81 to 100 shows the organization is a world-class Six Sigma organization.

Chapter

Profiles in
Six Sigma Leadership

■ SIX SIGMA LEADERSHIP

The last and most important element of the *A* in the $Q \times A = E$ formula is Six Sigma leadership. When all is said and done about Six Sigma, it is and always has been a management philosophy. This chapter discusses what is necessary to be a Six Sigma leader. We highlight methods to evaluate Six Sigma leadership skills and discuss how to improve the competencies of a Six Sigma leader. Finally, we address several brief sketches of Six Sigma leaders, from the Business Leader position to the more pivotal, yet important Quality Leader position.

■ THE SIX SIGMA LEADER

Embracing Six Sigma is more than just a tactical cost-savings initiative. Six Sigma is a management philosophy. It is a commitment to managing through *process*, not *function*, and making decisions based on fact and data rather than the inherent skills management believe make them great executives.

I have seen great executives fail at Six Sigma. I have also been fortunate to see great executives allow Six Sigma to make them even better executives.

■ SIX SIGMA LEADERSHIP CONCEPTS

To be a great Six Sigma executive, you must excel in the following areas:

➤ *Level of attention.* Put in the time required to change the way your business is managed. Move toward a process management philosophy rather than a functional alignment.

➤ *Charisma.* While many believe that charisma doesn't make a leader, I have yet to meet a successful Six Sigma executive who doesn't have charisma.

➤ *Challenging the status quo.* If you believe you can be a Six Sigma executive and not change the status quo of your business, you are fooling yourself.

➤ *Leading by example.* The concept behind GE's Green Belt for Champions course was that what is expected of the employee first, must be role modeled by the leaders of the organization. I have yet to see a successful Six Sigma company who didn't role model their skills in this first Six Sigma type experience.

■ SIX SIGMA LEADERSHIP SPECIFICS

A careful reading of both *The Six Sigma Revolution* and this book, *Making Six Sigma Last,* chronicles the specific elements of what a Six Sigma leader must do. Relative to the specifics they include:

1. Publicly committing his or her organization to a Six Sigma initiative.

2. Willingness to commit the resources to implement a companywide initiative.

3. Taking the time both to create and maintain a Business Process Management System.

4. Creating and participating in the ongoing work of a Business Quality Council, preferably making the staff meeting and the Business Quality Council one and the same.

5. Committing to the creation of a Six Sigma infrastructure that includes hiring the best and brightest for the Quality Leader and Master Black Belt positions.

6. Support for and involvement in Six Sigma training and Six Sigma projects, including role modeling project involvement through a Green Belt for Champions type course (see specifics in Chapter 5).

7. Motivating and managing project Champions so that each project created has a business leader competent to strategically lead the project to completion.

8. Commitment to hiring the best external consultants, not the cheapest.

9. Involvement in creating the need for Six Sigma for the organization.

10. Involvement in shaping the vision of what Six Sigma will be for their organization and detailing the results and behaviors of a Six Sigma organization.

11. Involvement in mobilizing commitment and personal involvement in diagnosing resistance and

inspiring others to change their current level of support for Six Sigma.

12. Consciously measuring the Six Sigma culture and taking appropriate corrective action.

13. Modifying the systems and structures of the organization such that Six Sigma thrives and grows.

14. Not allowing the Six Sigma initiative to be diluted by other initiatives.

■ SIX SIGMA LEADERSHIP MEASUREMENT (SELF / PEER / SUBORDINANT EVALUATIONS)

Virtually all executives think they are better managers than they really are. In years past, while managing a supplier development organization, I thought I was an excellent manager. I then instituted quarterly subordinate reviews only to find out that my staff didn't share in my perception that I was that good.

I did find these reviews of value to learn what was important to the people who reported to me. For example, during one quarterly review I received feedback that I was not as available to my people as they desired. When I asked for specifics, one of my staff members said, "You return client calls within 24 hours, but when I call you on the road, I often don't know when you will call back. How about returning our calls with the same urgency as you do clients'."

This feedback and suggestion for improvement ultimately made me a better manager. I suggest a similar approach to executives who want feedback on their current level of leadership and what corrective action needs to occur for them to be better Six Sigma leaders.

The tool to accomplish this feedback loop is a simple evaluation form, sent anonymously to key peers, subordinates, and if appropriate, to superiors. The most important respondent is the self review. The executive is often a tougher grader than peers, superiors, or even subordinates. Figure 7.1 shows a typical Six Sigma leadership evaluation, though there are variations of this form that are used by various executives depending on where they are in their implementation efforts.

It is common practice for this evaluation form to be sent to a sampling of the peers, subordinates, and in some cases, superiors. You will note there is an "other" category. In some cases, I have been asked to fill out such a form for an executive. Though for most clients, I have an arrangement whereby I provide direct feedback delivered one on one rather then through a formal written method.

The person who should coordinate these executive review sessions is the Quality Leader. The Quality Leader should be a trusted advisor for the executive staff. If there is hesitancy in having the Quality Leader provide this service, I become suspicious of the commitment of executive leadership, the skills of the Quality Leader, or both. Second, by coordinating the evaluations, the Quality Leader will be directly involved in the needed corrective actions. Figure 7.1 encompasses all of the necessary elements of Six Sigma leadership, however, it can be modified to meet the needs of a specific organization.

I encourage executives to begin these peer reviews sometime during the first wave of projects. In the first year of Six Sigma implementation, I recommend these peer reviews be administered a minimum of every three months. Further, I suggest that once the Quality Leader receives these evaluations back from peers, subordinates, and superiors (if applicable),

Element	Peer (1–5)	Subordinate (1–5)	Superior (1–5)	Other	Comments*
Has publicly and enthusiastically committed to Six Sigma in the organization.					
Has committed the resources sufficient for the Six Sigma initiative to be successful.					
Has created a Business Process Management system.					
Has maintained a Business Process Management system.					
Attends business quality council meetings regularly and participates accordingly.					
Has created a Six Sigma infrastructure populated with talent.					
Has involved themselves in Six Sigma training.					
Supports Six Sigma training for others.					

*Please include things done well that should continue for higher ratings/suggestions for improvement for lower ratings.

Figure 7.1 Elements of Six Sigma Leadership

the Quality Leader does a rollup of the evaluations. Furthermore, formal corrective action plans should be developed with the executive in question for any rating averaging less than three (on the Likert Scale of 1–5).

The Quality Leader must handle the first evaluation rollups with political sensitivity. The first time these evaluations are completed, I strongly encourage the Quality Leader to sit down briefly with each person filling out the form. In this brief discussion, I coach the Quality Leader to make sure the last column is filled out in detail. Elements that a given executive is doing well must be noted. First, development of new skills need to be recognized so that these skills are reinforced and strengthened. Second, many times an executive is unaware of what they are doing well. If these strengths are pinpointed, they increase the likelihood of occurring in the future.

Further, the Quality Leader should spend time discussing how to provide constructive criticism. Changing your management philosophy from one based on functional hierarchies versus process management is a difficult challenge for anyone, but particularly difficult for those who have succeeded using a management methodology that Six Sigma attempts to replace. Many executives have succeeded through management intuition. Six Sigma attempts to replace that approach with a management philosophy based on fact-based decision making. Thus, executives cannot be expected to change overnight. Feedback of a corrective type must be unequivocally stated. Moreover, specific, behavioral recommendations for improvement must always be stated.

Two examples of comments from peer evaluations for one of my executive clients follow. Our first example is a peer review for a business leader that is not productive. It does not further the effort for corrective action. Selective comments were:

Selected comments—Respondent 1:

➤ "Has not enthusiastically committed to Six Sigma."

➤ "Has not committed the resources sufficient for the Six Sigma initiative to be successful."

➤ "Has supported project Champions well."

This feedback is virtually useless. For feedback to be of value, it needs to be specific, measurable, and in the case where improvement is needed, suggestions for change should be clearly stated. This is not the case here. Imagine yourself receiving this feedback. Its purpose seems more to be to irritate rather than to help. Even in the case of positive feedback, there are no specifics. The last comment claims the executive is doing well on project Champion support. Yet, it doesn't say exactly what the executive is doing well, so that these new skills can be turned into habits.

Now compare the evaluation of this same executive from a different respondent, who feels essentially the same way as the previous respondent:

Selected comments—Respondent 2:

➤ "After the initial Six Sigma kick-off, this executive has missed several opportunities to publicly show her commitment to Six Sigma. For example, our recent all-manager meeting came and went without any mention of Six Sigma progress."

➤ "The current ratio of one Master Black Belt for seven projects creates the impression we are not supporting

Six Sigma. The Master Black Belt assigned to my project has missed nearly 50 percent of the meetings he has been invited to."

➤ "On the plus side, this executive has provided extensive training to Champions. They are competent to lead projects. I would recommend more questions asked of Champions during Business Quality Council meetings."

➤ "Has created a Six Sigma infrastructure populated with talent. Both the Quality Leader and Master Black Belts have exceeded my requirements talent-wise (when they are available, see above). I believe we can be totally self-reliant on our internal resources by the end of the year."

This is feedback that is both specific and useful, whether the feedback is positive or constructive. Both respondents believe the executive in question could improve supporting Six Sigma. But instead of just restating the question, the second respondent provided detailed information as to what prompted his low rating and a suggestion to raise the number by the time of the next rating. *"After the initial Six Sigma kick-off, this executive missed several opportunities to publicly show their commitment to Six Sigma. For example, our recent all-managers' meeting came and went without any mention of Six Sigma progress."*

With specific feedback, the executive is not only told what specific venue prompted his rating, but in doing so provides a specific suggestion (i.e., provide a Six Sigma update as part of every all-managers' meeting) to improve performance.

Respondent 1 feels his executive isn't providing enough resources to support Six Sigma. Respondent 2 feels the same way but communicates this feedback in a manner that may actually modify resource allocation. *"The current ratio of one Master Black Belt for seven projects creates the impression we are not supporting Six Sigma. The Master Black Belt assigned to my project has missed nearly 50 percent of the meetings he has been invited to."* This feedback is superb in several areas. It provides specificity with regard to deficiencies in resource allocation. Moreover, note the beauty of data. This feedback not once, but twice, references data to show that resource allocation is not what it should be. This type of feedback personifies the Six Sigma culture. Making decisions based on fact and data is what Six Sigma is all about. Getting people to use fact and data in how they communicate to one another is a sign of a Six Sigma culture transformation.

■ PROFILES IN SIX SIGMA LEADERSHIP COURAGE

There have been several individuals whom I have encountered who made implementing Six Sigma fun. While I am not a golfer, I have compared being a Six Sigma consultant to the joys and frustrations of golf. I have a friend named Dave. He's an avid golfer and once explained to me why he golfs. "I slice one shot, I miss an easy putt, I chip into a water hazard, and I want to give up the game. Then I drive two hundred yards, chip onto the green, tap in for a birdie, and I know I'll never give up the game."

Like Dave, I often feel the same way when helping organizations implement Six Sigma. Next is a sample of some of the better leaders who I have encountered relative to Six Sigma.

➤ Perry Monych

In Chapter 6, I referenced GE Access and mentioned how Perry Monych showed the leadership necessary to commit his organization to Six Sigma. There are many litmus tests I perform, some known, some unknown to the recipient of the test. Perry Monych is the only Business Leader who has passed every test.

One clear test of support to Six Sigma is how much time the Business Leader spends on the initiative. In the 1980s, I worked on a non-Six Sigma project with Xerox and was told this interesting story. At the beginning of the decade, the company produced manufactured copiers for what their Japanese competition sold theirs. This prompted their then CEO, David Kearns, to commit to winning the Malcolm Baldrige Award, perhaps the most prominent quality strategy in the decade of the 1980s. Kearns was serious about transforming his organization and he thought commitment to following the tenants that go toward winning the Baldrige Award would assist in changing Xerox for the better.

The process of winning the Baldrige Award is based on filing a detailed application about the various components of the organization's quality activities which, if warranted, leads to the finalists for the award receiving a site visit. These site visits conducted by a host of qualified site examiners who then determine who will win the Baldrige Award. A host of categories, from manufacturing to service organizations, to small business are recognized.

In the early 1980s, David Kearns unleashed his Baldrige initiative. He committed millions to training and consulting in an effort to win the Baldrige Award. Nearly a year later, Xerox was notified not even a site visit was forthcoming. At his next staff meeting, he is said to have engaged in a tirade about the lack of results toward winning the Baldrige Award. In the middle of this tirade, one of his direct reports asked him to get out his daily planner. Kearns did so. This direct report then asked him to review how much time Kearns had personally spent on leading the Baldrige Award effort. This brave direct report had nailed a key element of both Baldrige Award attainment and, coincidentally, Six Sigma implementation. This calendar check proved worthwhile. Xerox did go on to win the Baldrige Award in the late 1980s.

I bring this up to contrast the management style of Perry Monych. Once Perry vocalized his commitment to Six Sigma, an examination of his calendar would show he committed both time and resources to the job. Perry and his staff signed up for the Green Belt for Champions Training. Perry was an active participant. He helped to create their Six Sigma Business Process Management System and involved himself in all aspects of the training. Perhaps the most telling episode of his public support for Six Sigma was sitting in for two days of Change Management training. I could see him silently mouthing (as if a good cheerleader) many of the concepts I was teaching him. When I quoted Dave Schulenberg's famous quote "Customers feel variation, not averages," Perry was finishing the sentence out loud. Mid-day I asked him if he had been exposed to Change Management theory in the past.

"Oh yes, George, this is the third time I've taken the course."

"But, Perry," I exclaimed, "I would have understood if you missed two days of training you have taken before."

"Ah, my friend," Perry exhorted, "First, I am picking up concepts that I missed the first two times. Second, this is supposed to be Six Sigma management training. Even if it was a rehash of what I already know, it's like going to church, it's good for you. Going further, you are tying the change model to Six Sigma and I like how you're doing it. Finally, what kind of leader would I be if I didn't set a tone for mandatory attendance?"

This element of leading by participating is a hallmark of Monych's management style. Shortly after taking over from John Ramsey, he auctioned off his time for charity. As a result, Perry did various manual labor jobs to get to know all aspects of the new business he had taken on.

It's this type of participation that showed itself in both the strategic and tactical elements of Six Sigma. After his initial process management creation, he soon became interested in projects on a detailed, tactical level. Finally, as we referenced in Chapter 6, he tackled the difficult assignment of making a change in his Quality Leadership.

My dearly departed mother used to say to me, "Integrity is doing the right things when no one is watching." Perry has integrity. Toward the end of the tenure of his first Quality Leader, he shared with that person that he and I had been talking about me being a possible replacement. This led to an honest and respectful exchange between the Quality Leader and myself with everything being out in the open and being resolved in a highly dignified manner.

This honesty expanded to his Six Sigma work. When it came time to think of someone to write the Foreword of my first book, *The Six Sigma Revolution,* my first thoughts centered on Perry. His first impression was one of being honored but then he indicated that he didn't feel GE Access was of sufficient caliber of Six Sigma results for him to be bestowed the honor. After I used all of my negotiating skills, Perry finally relented and wrote a great Foreword for my first book.

In addition to having to make unpleasant managerial moves like transitioning his old Quality Leader out of his position, Perry clearly can engage in authoritarian leadership when the opportunity arises. As I have indicated, GE Access's management is among the best and brightest I have had the pleasure of working with. However, in the third month of training at the Boulderado Hotel in Boulder, Colorado, selected management decided to have a "Whine party." "Six Sigma is too cumbersome." "We are different. Six Sigma applies more to other General Electric businesses, but not to this one."

While Perry is the type of leader who encourages input and doesn't punish those who talk directly, on this day he had heard enough. Perry admonished his staff, indicated his commitment to Six Sigma, and indicated to his staff they could lead, follow, or get out of the way. While his closing statements that day were later criticized by a few as being too harsh, he had clearly set the expectations for his staff relative to Six Sigma. It is no coincidence that from that point on, we didn't experience problems with management support.

➤ Mike Delaney

It is with some irony that Mike Delaney is considered a world-class Six Sigma leader. At first glance, that may seem insulting to Mike, but no offense is intended. What I am referring to is Mike's chosen profession, marketing and strategic planning.

It is common knowledge among the quality consultant world that sales and marketing specialists are typically the last function to overcome their resistance. It was with some surprise, then, that I met Mike Delaney in 1996. At that time, Mike was working in marketing at GE Capital TIP (Transportation International Pool). If you spend any time on the road, you have seen their white truck trailers with their ubiquitous orange and black logos. I remember during Six Sigma overview training hearing a litany of questions from Mike. People who ask lots of questions can either be intellectually curious or using questions as a form of resistance. I plead guilty to prejudgment with Mike. Knowing his function, my original opinion was that he was trying to bait me into giving some wrong answer.

In hindsight, Mike Delaney's questions were fair, intelligent, and probing, much like his personality. Within weeks, Mike had established himself as a premier project sponsor, (the Champion in GE parlance) and a leader within GE TIP for Six Sigma.

By 1997, Mike had moved on to Volvo Trucks North America as vice president of marketing where one of his first tasks was to create the Six Sigma momentum within his organization. Mike's sales and marketing skills are paramount. I know from personal experience. As the demand for Six Sigma has grown, I no longer feel compelled to be flexible in my approach. I strongly encourage each business to begin strategically with creation of the Business Process Management System. Thus, when Mike asked me to do a series of Project Improvement Training Sessions for five Six Sigma pilot projects that he would personally Champion, I was hesitant to agree. Because his sales skills were beyond my level of resistance, I agreed to conduct this first wave of pilot projects. I am glad I did. I had predicted two of the five projects to be clear winners, one project would be a close call, and two others would be learning exercises at best.

To be operationally defined a success, both sigma performance and a significant cost savings should be generated. Most successful projects average between $150,000 to

$175,000 in cost savings. Of course, the return on investment may be less, dependent on the type of project you select and the degree of success you achieve.

Due to the strategic leadership of Mike Delaney and the tactical support of Volvo's Six Sigma leader (Bill Brubaker), virtually all of Volvo's first projects were significant successes. A truck modification project generated over $1 million in cost savings. Another Volvo Trucks project succeeded in improving their forecasting process which has untold financial impact to the business. On the manufacturing side of the house, a fuel placement project significantly reduced fuel tank replacement down time.

While a host of people contribute to the success of the projects, Mike Delaney's support cannot be underestimated. Throughout his training and experience at GE Capital TIP, Mike not only knew the concepts, but the detailed math associated with Six Sigma. When a Black Belt comes before Mike Delaney in his role of Champion, he or she must be prepared for detailed questions and be expected to deliver pertinent, detailed answers. Further, if Mike Delaney is your Champion, expect to see him on a regular basis. Despite my encouragement to the contrary, many Champions end up giving only cursory interest to Six Sigma. With Mike, you will be seeing him early and often.

Despite all these strengths of Mike Delaney, I haven't discussed his greatest Six Sigma strength. Earlier in this chapter I showed an example of an individual who used facts and data in an everyday setting, thus personifying Six Sigma as a cultural phenomenon.

No one better personifies the concept of making Six Sigma philosophy an everyday behavior than Mike Delaney. Now as Vice President of Marketing and Strategic Planning for Unifi, a major North Carolina textile manufacturer, Mike rarely makes a decision without someone showing him the data. He is not persuaded with an anecdote. What does the hard data reveal? Show him a Pareto chart or a histogram to influence him. As he once aptly pointed out, "Without data, you are just another person with an opinion." Mike simply will not make a process change without showing him the data.

Mike also sees what many people don't. When done right, Six Sigma becomes a potent secondary marketing strategy. In his current position with Unifi, he has already started to use Six Sigma success as a vehicle for obtaining contracts.

➤ Jack Becker

There is a scene in the movie *Body Heat,* where William Hurt is asking Mickey Rourke for information about arson. Mickey Rourke is hesitant and is trying to talk William Hurt out of his potential criminal activity. "Think about this long and hard," he warns Hurt's character, "There are a thousand ways in which you can screw up and a genius will think of a hundred."

Later I heard Deming give a variation on Rourke's line. Deming once said that a project improvement team should ask a thousand questions about their work and a genius will think of a hundred questions.

When I think of Deming's comments on asking questions, I think of Jack Becker. Jack has asked me more questions about Six Sigma than any one person. Technical questions, strategic questions, tactical questions, hiring questions, and the like are a part of the intellectual curiosity that has contributed to Jack Becker being one of the best Quality Leaders I have encountered.

Jack Becker has been the Quality Leader for Lithonia Lighting based in Conyers, Georgia, since the position was created in 1999. Jack personifies the myriad qualities I reference in Chapter 5 about the Quality Leader.

First, he was an internal hire with a long history of accomplishment for Lithonia Lighting. Jack has been an employee of Lithonia since 1976. After first starting out as a manufacturing manager, he quickly rose through the ranks and was promoted to director of operations in 1987. Lithonia Lighting experienced significant growth during the time of Jack's tenure. Among his many accomplishments was maintaining the highest operating margins in the company, taking the oldest and most unproductive unionized plant in the company and doubling its productivity in 18 months.

During his time in operations, he had always been prone to examining new ideas and experimenting with new approaches to improving Lithonia's culture. In the 1980s, being influenced by Richard Schoenberger's book *World Class Manufacturing,* he incorporated a production system that maintained high-quality levels while demand was growing at 30 percent a year for over five years.

The initial success of implementing a Schoenberger-like manufacturing system whetted his appetite for an approach that could be more strategic and companywide. He developed a reputation for challenging the status quo and for being a change agent.

Former Senator Sam Nunn is on the Lithonia Lighting Board of Directors. Among Senator Nunn's other commitments is being on the Board of Directors of General Electric. Seeing the impact Six Sigma had on General Electric, it was only natural that Nunn would advocate a similar approach at Lithonia. Knowing the importance of selecting the best and brightest, Jack Becker was chosen as the Vice President of Six Sigma.

The biggest compliment I can give Jack is that whenever he asked for an evening to discuss Six Sigma, I know that it will be thought-provoking and challenging. While eating at our favorite Conyers restaurant, Michelangelo's, one night I turned the tables on Jack and asked him questions.

Among the first questions I asked him was why he thought he was chosen as Lithonia's Quality Leader. "I was told I was willing to be politically incorrect and tell the emperor he was naked." Of course, Jack was also told he had the ability to think both strategically and tactically, gain support for new initiatives, and was respected throughout the organization.

I have seen no Quality Leader better able to balance being an advocate for Six Sigma among his fellow executives and middle management and still be able to take the pulse of the culture and back off pushing when he thought he might push an executive into what Jack Becker calls "permanent resistance."

Jack shared an interesting story that night about Lithonia's initial commitment to Six Sigma. Despite the strong encouragement of Sam Nunn, there were executives that didn't like the potential negative impact on the Profit and Loss Statement for upwards of a year. Jack worked with the more receptive executives of his executive leadership team (ELT) to build alliances among the more reluctant executives on his team. These alliances forged his first major victory when Lithonia made a major investment in their first year of Six Sigma implementation.

He also practiced many of the concepts found in this book before he was exposed to them. In Chapter 3, we discussed cultural resistance and how to combat it. In that chapter, we talked of modifying the initiative when faced with cultural resistance. That was the case when Lithonia started their Six Sigma effort. Hiring a General Electric division that specializes in Six Sigma consulting, Lithonia modified their approach by excluding the Business Process Management elements initially. Jack had made this modification in order to gain greater acceptance on the part of the more reluctant executives on the ELT.

Business Process Management wasn't abandoned. Instead, Jack got agreement to start two waves of process improvement DMAIC training as "show me" projects to the more reluctant executives with the understanding that Business Process Management would be the priority in the second year of Lithonia's Six Sigma effort. While risky (and not what I would have recommended), the strategy worked. General Electric asked me to provide the training piece for the first wave of training and multiple successes ensued.

As Jack said about his strategy, "We took this approach and worked hard to make sure that projects were selected with a clear understanding of their potential impact on the ELT and the business objectives. The approach worked and the ELT has now committed to deploying the Business Process Management elements during our second year of deployment."

■ FINAL THOUGHTS ON SIX SIGMA LEADERSHIP

As the keynote speaker at a Sun Microsystems information conference recently, I was asked what was the one key difference between Six Sigma and other quality efforts that have come before it. Having participated in many of these previous efforts, it wasn't a hard question to answer. Long will I remember working tactical projects using many of the same tools I now teach as part of Six Sigma. To me, the biggest difference has been the more strategic involvement of the business leaders of an organization. I would be remiss if, in this chapter on Six Sigma leadership, I didn't mention the three Business Leaders who have had the biggest impact on verifying my claim that Six Sigma is different than other initiatives: Bob Galvin of Motorola, Lawrence Bossidy of AlliedSignal, and Jack Welch of General Electric.

Without the leadership of Bob Galvin, there would be no Six Sigma. While Mikel Harry was the driver that created the concept of Six Sigma at Motorola and should be given significant credit for selling Six Sigma to Bob Galvin, it was Galvin himself who made Six Sigma a management philosophy. He exhorted his employees from his direct reports to individual contributors to practice the philosophy of never-ending improvement through Six Sigma methodology. I remember his 1992 keynote speech at the Juran Institute where his enthusiasm for Six Sigma was palpable. What I remember most about this moment was that it was the first time in my memory that a CEO was advocating a quality approach. It was then that I realized that Six Sigma was going to be different.

Even with Galvin's wholehearted support for Six Sigma, it was probably Lawrence Bossidy that made Six Sigma more than an initiative unique to Motorola. In a bold and decisive move, Bossidy embraced Six Sigma shortly after taking over AlliedSignal. The significant impact Six Sigma made in AlliedSignal showed it not to be a Motorola unique phenomenon. Bossidy, a former General Electric executive who left to take over Allied in 1991, kept close contact with his former boss and friend, Jack Welch. It was Bossidy's success at Allied that prompted a summer 1995 seminar at

General Electric, while Jack Welch was recovering from surgery. By that fall, Jack Welch was a convert, saying Six Sigma was the most important initiative that he had ever undertaken.

Volumes of books have been written about Jack Welch. Managing change in a company as large as General Electric can be like turning an aircraft carrier around in a different direction. With Jack Welch at the helm, it became clear that he was serious about Six Sigma when he dictated that 40 percent of each manager's bonus would be dependent on his Six Sigma performance.

Without these three business leaders, Six Sigma would not be the worldwide management philosophy it has become.

■ SUMMARY

Leadership is a critical success factor for the culture of Six Sigma to take root. In this chapter, we reviewed both general and specific Six Sigma leadership traits. We then reviewed how to formally collect data on how well your executive leadership team is doing against the specific leadership traits. Peer, subordinate, and superior evaluations were reviewed. How to take these reviews and improve an executives' Six Sigma leadership behaviors were covered.

In the last part of the chapter we met several Six Sigma leaders, both at the executive level and within the quality arena.

KEY LEARNINGS

➤ A Six Sigma leader must master skills relative to both the Q and the A of Six Sigma.

➤ Formal reviews of leaders should begin before the first year of Six Sigma implementation.

➤ The Quality Leader should manage this review process.

➤ Leadership reviews must result in specific, measurable feedback whether the feedback is positive or constructive criticism.

➤ Profiles of several key Six Sigma leaders show that leadership of Six Sigma must be behavorial, not verbal. Among the best of these individuals are Perry Monych, Mike Delaney, and Jack Becker.

Chapter 8

Pitfalls to Avoid in Creating the Six Sigma Culture

In our final chapter, we review common pitfalls that await the organization trying to implement Six Sigma. Like in my first book, *The Six Sigma Revolution,* our last chapter is devoted to the common pitfalls that can derail the best intentions if not managed properly.

At first glance, you may think that avoiding many of these pitfalls is just common sense. Since pitfalls are seen time and again by consultants, the old adage that common sense is not that common must be true.

■ PITFALL 1—FAILURE TO ACHIEVE QUICK SUCCESSES

In 1993, Bay Networks, a Silicon Valley software peripherals organization, hired me to work on supplier development at the tactical level. As such, I worked on various projects associated with the Design of Experiments tool of Six Sigma. In August of that year, Bay Networks was experiencing quality problems with a single source of material in Texas, Honeywell Microswitch. A normally reliable source, as can be the case with computer products, the recipe seemed to have been lost.

Dennis Omanoff and Dave Cook, two prominent Quality Leaders at Bay Networks, asked me to visit Richardson, Texas, and begin work with them to design a series of experiments to restore Honeywell's excellent quality rating.

Dave Cook, Deanna VanWestenberg (a quality engineer at Bay Networks), and I visited Honeywell late in August. Long will I remember the first morning when, despite Dave Cook's gracious introduction of me, I faced a group of 12 to 15 engineers who seemed to personify organizational resistance. Dave said that they were to follow my recommendations as if I were the customer. This did not go over well. To Honeywell, I was the expert from out of town, and as such what did I know about their business.

What they didn't know was that my recommendations were to teach them a portion of the Six Sigma methodology to better use *their* expertise. I knew that I had to make a quick and dramatic impact if I were to survive. I taught an abbreviated and modified Design of Experiments course over the next three days and proceeded with Dave and Deanna's help, set up three different experiments to identify factors contributing to the unusually high defect rate.

While I returned a few times over the next three months, Dave Cook visited the facility weekly and worked with competent Honeywell personnel like Bobby Hawthorne and Sogand Shodja to drive the Bay Networks defect rate down from 46 percent when we started the project to less than 2 percent. Certainly not Six Sigma quality, but Honeywell's reputation as a preferred supplier returned.

As a direct result of this success, Honeywell Microswitch became zealots about Designed Experiments. They had me return multiple times throughout the next year, and each visit was more enjoyable than the previous one. Honeywell treated me with tremendous respect which clearly would not have been the case if that first major project had not been not successful.

I don't recommend pinning your Six Sigma hopes on just one project. Through good process management, high-impact projects will be selected for the first wave of Six Sigma training (see Chapter 2 of *The Six Sigma Revolution*). A significant percentage of these first high-impact projects, however, must bear fruit. I have come to call these first-wave Six Sigma projects the "show me" projects. They are the first opportunities for the organization to begin driving improvement, so they also play an important cultural factor in showing skeptics that Six Sigma can work in their organization. While I teach using a host of examples from various organizations, I have come to the strong conclusion that until there are first successes within the organization in question, true commitment to Six Sigma will not occur.

In virtually 100 percent of the Six Sigma clients that have true cultural transformation, the first wave of projects produced significant results. Thus, once the projects are selected as part of the beginning work of the Business Process Management System, I strongly encourage a level of micromanagement on the part of the project by Champions so that these projects stand the greatest chance of success. Once these first-wave projects are completed, the level of micromanagement can be reduced. But without significant and tangible success, the enemies of Six Sigma within an organization will have substantial ammunition to begin recruiting people to their side.

Once these quick successes have occurred, they need to be communicated early, often, and loudly. In Chapter 7, we discussed the significant "quick hits" that Volvo Trucks North America generated in their pilot programs under the leadership of Mike Delaney and Bill Brubaker. Shortly after most of these successes were generated, Mike Delaney went on to take the marketing and strategic planning post at Unifi. Nearly a year later, upper management did not have an appreciation of the impact of these projects. It was only when Bill Brubaker presented the successes during the next wave of project selection that management began to see the power of Six Sigma. It was not a question of them not being informed, but it took a great presentation by Bill to really sway some of the doubters at Volvo Trucks.

■ PITFALL 2—CLEAR YOUR AGENDAS OF COMPETING DISTRACTIONS

In the late 1980s, I became certified as a ISO-9000 assessor, recognizing as a consultant that ISO-9000 was becoming increasingly popular. Trained by competent and seasoned experts at the British Standards Institute, I began marketing my consulting with ISO-9000 as part of my service offerings.

Very quickly I became skeptical (skepticism is resistance when you are talking about yourself) when, in the first few years of consulting, I began thinking ISO was more documentation than improvement. In the early 1990s I dropped ISO consulting from my services, knowing that if a consultant is to be any good, he must be an evangelist for his services.

I am sure that there are a host of organizations that have profited from their certification by the ISO standards. I use ISO to highlight Pitfall 2, which states you must clear all your agendas of competing distractions. What I mean by this is many business leaders rely too heavily on the latest fad. Yes, I have no doubts that many organizations are now using Six Sigma in the way many organizations used Malcolm Baldrige and ISO-9000 in years past.

If you choose Baldrige or ISO-9000, good for you. While I have my personal views on ISO (and Baldrige, for that matter), commit to these philosophies and implement them fully. However, if you commit to Six Sigma, it cannot be in conjunction with other programs or initiatives.

While I mentioned Baldrige and ISO, I don't mean to pick on these as your only distractions. When done comprehensively, Six Sigma can incorporate many other themes as part of improvement. However, I have become sensitive to the individual contributor of an organization who, when first introduced to Six Sigma, thinks it's the "flavor of the month." For several years I thought these comments were the excuse used by organizational resistors. While that may be the case, I have now concluded that employees are sometimes bombarded with new initiatives and if these new initiatives are combined with Six Sigma at the same time, you can expect problems among the rank and file.

In discussions with several of my clients who have been ISO registered for several years, I have suggested to them that they quietly drop their registration. In the case of ISO, yearly audits require significant manpower to implement corrective actions and update documentation. If you are focused on these efforts and then are told to participate in Six Sigma project work or process management, it is no wonder that so many consultants hear the refrain, "I have my regular job and all these initiatives besides."

It should be noted that in some cases, multiple initiatives are not distractions and, in fact, nicely build on one another. I believe that is the case at General Electric. Ironically, no other business I have ever have worked with has had more initiatives than General Electric. However, many of them have built on one another to create the rationale that led to Six Sigma.

Beth Galucci, the noted General Electric expert of change, has a page in her Change Acceleration Process course that she has dubbed "The Stairway to Heaven" chart (with all due respect to Led Zeppelin). "The Stairway to Heaven" charts the initiatives that Jack Welch has spearheaded since the 1980s to the arrival of Six Sigma in 1995. One of the first major initiatives in the 1980s for General Electric was "Work-Out," a bureaucracy busting, proactive methodology that empowers employees to quickly define problems and analyze and recommend solutions for troubled areas in a organization. Dubbed "Six Sigma Lite" by pessimists, you can see that elements of the Six Sigma DMAIC steps (the Define, Analyze and Improve sections) are included in Work-Out. My first consulting work for General Electric was as a facilitator for Work-Out, assisting the Destra Consulting Group with several of their Work-Out contracts.

"Best Practices" was a method to benchmark how other departments or other organizations were doing something well. This clearly is a theme of Six Sigma because many times the improvements to improve sigma performance come from studying previous projects, both within an organization and beyond.

In the early 1990s, in an attempt to bolster the relative absence of measurement in Work-Out, process improvement was introduced at GE. Again, you can see a pattern developing among the various initiatives. Work-out was still the domain for more administrative problems, but now process improvement began to address more manufacturing concerns and those areas where measurement was pivotal to improvement.

Less known but still important initiatives followed until Six Sigma's arrival in 1995. To the jaded, these are a series of independent initiatives. However, even my cursory examination shows similarities and interconnectedness among them. Therefore, we are not advocating Six Sigma exclusively. Yet, a major roadblock in the path of successful Six Sigma implementation are distractions. Keep them to a minimum.

■ PITFALL 3—UNREALISTIC TIME FRAMES

As Dick Benson, the former Business Leader of Fujitsu of America, has posted in his office, "When you are through learning, you are through." Thus, in recent years, I have modified the time frame for Six Sigma cultural success.

If you define Six Sigma success as tactical return-on-investment cost savings, this should occur within a period of months. In this context, however, I am referring to the approximate 30 percent of my clients that have achieved a cultural transformation using Six Sigma as a management philosophy.

When Jack Welch asked Bob Galvin how long it took for Motorola to have Six Sigma as a cultural phenomenon, Mr. Galvin responded that the culture part took 10 years. Ever the competitor, Welch committed to having Six Sigma in 5 years at General Electric. A common question during General Electric Six Sigma training was if I thought this goal was too aggressive. Taking the safe way out (it is never wise to disagree with the Business Leader), I replied that I thought General Electric was capable of generating the greatest cost impact of any organization attempting Six Sigma implementation in 5 years, but a true Six Sigma culture for an organization as large as General Electric could take awhile. I will leave it to others to determine the time frame on General Electric's Six Sigma enculturation, however, I would not hesitate to tell any client that virtually all activities under the Six Sigma banner take longer than I thought they did originally.

For example, initially I would tell project teams that they should scope their work to be achieved in 90 to 120 days. Seeing hard-working teams push the envelope of work levels to achieve results in that time frame has altered my thoughts on the topic. I now think first projects should wrap up in 120 to 160 days.

The same expansion of time is needed to create and be able to manage your Business Process Management System. One root cause I have been able to attribute to this time frame issue is that while Six Sigma is my life, it took close to 20 years to become proficient in the various tools and techniques of Six Sigma. Sometimes I need to better appreciate the learning curve of someone learning Six Sigma, whether it is the strategic pieces or the tactical elements.

■ PITFALL 4—IGNORING PREVIOUS QUALITY EFFORTS

In the context of the Six Sigma culture, ignoring previous quality efforts can mean a strengthening of some resistance in the organization from the most unlikely sources, those involved in the quality arena.

Quality professionals are an unappreciated lot. In many cases, the way their discipline in the past has operated, it is not hard to see why. In years past, the quality function was focused on quality control where inspection was the name of the game. As such, many other employees either saw quality as a necessary evil or an unnecessary reality. As the quality function began to stress quality assurance in the 1980s, they were often ignored based on their inspection reputation. Many of these early efforts at quality assurance were important first steps that actually helped Six Sigma be as popular as it is today. In the early 1980s, my first experience in the quality field was teaching Statistical Process Control (SPC). SPC as a standalone will not transform a culture, but clearly is the foundation for the Control portion of the DMAIC methodology. Other examples exist, such as Designed Experiments (which is a considerable portion of the Analysis and Improve elements of DMAIC).

A mistake many organizations (and consultants) make is to ignore previous efforts as well as the individuals who were a part of that previous effort. It is imperative when implementing Six Sigma that, when possible, Six Sigma be molded around previous efforts. At Lithonia Lighting, their previous quality effort was renamed Q6. The symbolism is more than just renaming of their previous quality effort. It symbolically sends the message that their previous quality effort, while flawed, was not being abandoned, but now raised to the power of Six Sigma.

In addition to not ignoring previous quality efforts and molding the previous efforts into Six Sigma, it is important not to ignore the people from the previous effort. Incorporating quality professionals into the new Six Sigma effort is important not only to reduce resistance but also to learn what went wrong with the previous effort. While there is always the danger of having those associated with a previously failed effort impact Six Sigma progress, I still recommend that previous efforts not be ignored.

■ PITFALL 5—POOR SIX SIGMA CULTURAL PLANNING AND FOLLOW-THROUGH

It is common for all of us to play to our strengths. In typical organizations, most work is focused on the technical aspects of work. This book focuses on acceptance of Six Sigma.

Another major pitfall as it relates to the culture of Six Sigma is poor administration of its acceptance. Specifically, examination of most Six Sigma efforts show most of the time administrative planning is around the technical areas of implementation. Often, when consulting with a client, I will request to see their implementation plan for Six Sigma. Even after receiving training reflecting the concepts in this book, I rarely see the cultural component of Six Sigma implementation addressed in the implementation plan.

I have concluded that the reason behind this lack of cultural administration is how foreign it is as both concept and technique. It is one thing to start doing things to processes, but management of cultural acceptance of Six Sigma is "people work." To plan and implement cultural acceptance of Six Sigma means working the people side of the business, and this is daunting to most executives.

If your organization has a Six Sigma implementation plan, review it carefully for the elements centering around cultural planning and follow-through. A suggestion some of my clients have found helpful is to review the Six Sigma implementation plan (of course, this assumes you actually have a Six Sigma plan) and review each item as to whether the activity is a Q or an A. If there is significant imbalance toward Q, revision of the plan to have greater A balance is strongly recommended.

■ PITFALL 6—CULTURAL DEVELOPMENT CANNOT BE DELEGATED OR SEEN AS A ONE-TIME EVENT

Years ago, I was doing a Six Sigma overview for a potential client. The overview ended with a review of the key elements of Six Sigma change management, many of which are topics covered in this book. One of my skills in providing seminars is being able to "read my audience." This day it was difficult reading the CEO until the afternoon when I was reviewing the Six Sigma management change elements. This CEO's eyes brightened and he proceeded to ask several pertinent questions. By the time I ended the day, it was time to discuss next steps. I was encouraged by the CEO's interest in the cultural aspects of Six Sigma since this was atypical in an executive during the first discussion of Six Sigma. Then, the CEO looked at his Human Resource Vice President and said the following, "This Six Sigma culture seems important. Jack, as our HR person, I want you to go out and do this for us."

The comment floored me. This CEO was delegating the most important aspect of the Six Sigma management philosophy. Despite discussion about the CEO's role, this client did not end up being a Six Sigma success story.

In addition to recognizing that Six Sigma cultural development cannot be delegated, it is important to recognize that activities around Six Sigma cannot be a one-time event. Whether the activity is communicating Six Sigma or dealing with resistance, management must recognize that the acceptance of Six Sigma takes repeated interventions.

Let's examine a situation centering around resistance in which I exhibit the pitfall I am now telling you to avoid. The year is 1993 and I am working with a pharmaceutical company located in both the United States and Europe. My contract called for me to work with scientists in implementing improved productivity in their product releases. While this contract did not call for a complete Six Sigma implementation strategy, it did call for major restructuring of how these scientists conducted their work.

Having been a psychologist and having worked with physicians, I was aware of the "white coat" effect, a fancy name for doctors feeling they are gods. These research scientists were working on determining why a certain pharmaceutical product was losing its potency. I was teaching them various Six Sigma tools to assist them verify their theories as to why the medication was losing its potency.

Once we learned the root causation of the lost potency, I initially felt that we were going to have a dramatic success story. Through the use of such Six Sigma tools as Pareto analysis, cause-effect diagrams, and Designed Experiments, we were able to harness these scientists' brilliance to isolate why the medication had lost its potency and what we had to do to return it to its previous level.

As we discussed in *The Six Sigma Revolution* (Chapter 8), it is important to identify stakeholders that are affected by a project's set of solutions. Stakeholder analysis, like the type we discussed in Chapter 3, applies to project solution implementation. In the case of the pharmaceutical project, a key scientist's theory had been disproven by the data. In the implementation phase of the project, we needed this key scientist to sell our changed formula for the medication to his direct reports. Table 8.1 is the stakeholder analysis for this scientist.

This sample of the stakeholder analysis shows that Frank, the scientist, is moderately against the new formula

Key Stakeholder	Strongly Against	Moderately Against	Neutral	Moderately Supportive	Strongly Supportive
Frank, the key Scientist		O----------	------------------------	----------------------	-------X

Table 8.1   Stakeholder analysis.

despite the fact that there is data to support the new formula. Why? Frank had a vested interest in his pet theory and thus was exhibiting political resistance. You might remember from Chapter 3 that political resistance occurs when the stakeholder sees the new solution as loss. Here, Frank saw the new formula as loss of prestige of his stature, having committed to a theory that was disproved by our Six Sigma tools. Table 8.2 shows our strategy for trying to change Frank from being moderately against to being strongly supportive, where we need Frank to be if we are to be successful with the new formula.

With this strategy, we wanted Frank to see the value of the new formula by having him see his work as a contributor to the new formula.

I took the action item of convincing him of this contribution. I scheduled a meeting over lunch. The lunch went well. I informed him of the importance of the project, the great teamwork that transpired when we were applying the Six Sigma tools and his involvement on the team. I complimented his involvement and did my best to have Frank admit that the new formula would produce great results. Finally, after much prodding, I got what I came for when Frank said, "Yes, this new formula is great."

Type of Resistance	Underlying Issue	Strategy to Change the Resistance
Political	Loss of prestige	Have Frank see and be part of the work that created the new formula.

Table 8.2 Frank's stakeholder analysis.

With this proclamation, I concluded Frank was on board and I quickly called for the lunch check (yes, sometimes the consultant picks up the check, but not very often).

I reported back to the project team that Frank was on board and beamed with my apparent ability to move a resistor to a more supportive position.

I had made a large mistake. If I had dug deeper, I would have found a caveat to Frank's claim that the new formula was great. Sure, the new formula was great, but I hadn't had him renounce his previous theory. Frank went on to sabotage the new formula.

This story shows that in creating a Six Sigma culture you cannot expect one intervention to create what you need. You will either make a mistake about perceived commitment or think that you have what you want when more time is needed. Pitfall 6 means you will not have a Six Sigma culture by delegating nor by thinking one intervention will result in the desired result.

■ PITFALL 7—NO CULTURAL GOALS OR OBJECTIVES

Once an organization commits to Six Sigma as a management philosophy, certain goals and objectives around the Q can come alive. Much harder, but perhaps more important, is to have a set of cultural goals and objectives. I recommend the following as more important cultural objectives:

> ➤ *Movement of stakeholders to desired targets.* In Chapter 3, we examined the stakeholder analysis chart and saw how to track where a stakeholder is in relation to Six Sigma commitment and where they need to be. Good executives sometimes use a tracking sheet to see

how successful movement of resistors are to their desired targeted commitment.

➤ *Greater informal Six Sigma behaviors.* In Chapter 4, we discussed the vision, results, and behaviors of a Six Sigma culture. Several behaviors that indicate a Six Sigma culture include management by fact rather than decision making by anecdote. The management style of Mike Delaney (see Chapter 7) is a great example of informal Six Sigma behavior which reflects a desired cultural goal.

➤ *Commonality of message.* I know that a client is on their way to becoming a Six Sigma cultural transformation success story when I hear similar messages throughout the executive team. For example, when I hear the executive team giving the same answers during staff meetings as to the threats/opportunities that prompted the organization to pursue Six Sigma, or give the same elevator speech (see Chapter 4), then I know the organization is achieving more than just tactical results.

■ PITFALL 8—NOT ALLOWING FOR UNEXPECTED INTERRUPTIONS

In Chapter 2, we told you the story of StorageTek's 1984 Chapter 11 Bankruptcy filing. Clearly, this was an unexpected interruption on the path to quality improvement. While dramatic, other unexpected interruptions will always compete with Six Sigma for your time and attention.

For example, in virtually every Six Sigma roll out I have been a part of, I hear a litany of reasons why something can't be accomplished in the time frame allowed. When I start Black Belt training I repeatedly hear the same reasons behind delays in implementation. Among the more common reasons I have heard are:

➤ *Negative impact to the sales of the organization.* Rather than seeing the negative impact to sales as a short-term threat that creates the need for the Six Sigma culture, it sometimes is used as the reason behind not being more diligent in the pursuit of Six Sigma.

➤ *Impending layoffs.* I have had organizations claim they are not further along with their Six Sigma culture because of the impact of impending layoffs. I always stress the importance of honesty and integrity in dealing with other business factors that may coincide with Six Sigma implementation.

➤ *Holidays/Vacations.* As I indicated in my discussion on Black Belt training, I give each team a set of intersession work before I return for the next wave of training. When I give them their minimum, target, and stretch goals, I often hear reasons why it will be hard to complete their intersession work. In the summer, vacation time interrupts the work. In the fall, it is the upcoming holidays, and in the spring, it is more holidays.

➤ *Mergers/Acquisitions.* Many Six Sigma initiatives are done by organizations threatened with the possibility of being taken over by another company. In other cases, Six Sigma organizations are interested in taking over companies.

Whatever the reason behind the interruption, this should be a factor when thinking about factors that impact Six Sigma cultural transformation.

■ PITFALL 9—FALSE POSITIVE READINGS THAT YOU HAVE ACHIEVED SIX SIGMA CULTURAL TRANSFORMATION

In the late 1990s, there was a conference for the various consultants working with General Electric. During this conference a handful of the consultants gave various tutorials (I gave a tutorial on Business Process Management), and we had several meetings where we provided a status on various General Electric business units.

As is often the case in conferences like this, work was done during the dinners. At one dinner, another consultant described the apparent success of one General Electric business unit that had one of the more charismatic leaders that the consultant had worked with. Indeed, the more the consultant talked, the more I was impressed with the work of this consultant's client. They had clearly created a vibrant Business Process Management System. They clearly were managing processes, not functions. They had active process dashboards. They had generated significant cost savings on their first-wave projects. They had selected a nice blend of projects that reflected effectiveness and efficiency. The consultant beamed with justified pride that the business leader had generated considerable effort toward acceptance of Six Sigma.

When questioned by others at that dinner, the consultant described in detail how the business leader had personally involved himself in creating the need for Six Sigma, dealing personally with key stakeholders in regard to resistance. By the time dinner concluded, I had offered my deepest congratulations, knowing this consultant had experienced frustrations with other General Electric business units and that he needed to have a client like this.

Less than six months later in Atlanta's Hartsfield Airport, I ran into this consultant in one of the airline club rooms. The consultant described how the General Electric business unit he had described as a Six Sigma cultural transformation was now floundering in their effort.

"What happened," I asked?

"My Business Leader left," he replied, "and Six Sigma as a cultural entity left with him." Over a drink I bought him, he went on to describe how this Business Leader had been a true evangelist of Six Sigma. As it turns out, this evangelism sometimes went too far in the eyes of some of his direct reports. Later, when one of them replaced the Business Leader who had taken a promotion elsewhere in General Electric, the new Business Leader had scaled back the Six Sigma effort. The scale back was not so noticeable as to not be in compliance with General Electric expectations, but enough so that they were now an organization that was implementing Six Sigma tactically, no longer as a cultural phenomenon.

The key point behind this story is to be careful declaring victory too early. Often after planting, there is fruit that may make the tree look well-rooted, but a good wind can play havoc with your effort. In this case, there wasn't really a cultural transformation, it was a case of one person making it look like a cultural transformation.

■ PITFALL 10—UNDERESTIMATING RESOURCE ALLOCATION

When a client thinks of implementing Six Sigma, they tend to see the known costs of Process Management training, Black Belt training, and Master Black Belt development. One aspect of resource allocation for the cultural component that is often underestimated is ongoing consultant costs that should be budgeted to sustain the cultural component.

Many times an organization will budget for only the Q costs of Six Sigma and then later reduce the budget for A work. I have received the most modification on proposals around Six Sigma A costs. If it is a client I really want to work with, I will remove second- and third-year consulting costs on A, hoping to convince them through working with them that these later costs are justified.

I often have clients who in the first year asked for A money to come out of the budget say, "Why didn't you tell us we would need you for cultural consulting to begin with?'

■ SUMMARY

In this last chapter, we addressed some of the many pitfalls that may occur using real cases to illustrate as necessary.

KEY LEARNINGS

Some of the pitfalls that await an organization in creating the Six Sigma culture include:

➤ Pitfall 1—Failure to Achieve Quick Successes.

➤ Pitfall 2—Clear Your Agenda of Competing Distractions.

➤ Pitfall 3—Unrealistic Time Frames.

➤ Pitfall 4—Ignoring Previous Quality Efforts.

➤ Pitfall 5—Poor Six Sigma Cultural Planning and Follow-Through.

(continued)

(Continued)

➤ Pitfall 6—Cultural Development Cannot Be Delegated or Seen as a One-Time Event.

➤ Pitfall 7—No Cultural Goals or Objectives.

➤ Pitfall 8—Not Allowing for Unexpected Interruptions.

➤ Pitfall 9—False Positive Readings That You Have Achieved Six Sigma Cultural Transformation.

➤ Pitfall 10—Underestimating Resource Allocation.

Last Thoughts

Making Six Sigma Last may be the most important book you read. While the techniques, tools, and strategies of Six Sigma can result in tremendous increases in productivity, the odds of this occurring without implementing the practical ideas in this book are small.

If your effort to implement Six Sigma is faltering, then it is incumbent upon you and your organization to practice the skills in this book to gain greater acceptance. Creating a Six Sigma culture can be your greatest legacy in being a business leader. Good luck to you.

Index